# Book III
The Great Persian Saga Continues
# The Delphic Oracle

By Dr. Jeffrey Donner

PYTHIA

ISBN: 978-1-7320143-2-9

GRAECIA
ANTIQVA

Delphi

Athens

Corinth

Aegina

# The Players

## The Persians

Xerxes- King of Kings- ruler of the Great Persian Empire

Artemisia- Warrior Queen of Halicarnassus

Hamas- the "teacher" of Xerxes

Adon- Phoenician bodyguard of Artemisia

Ningizzida- Rogue priest- most powerful priest in Empire

Ummanaldash- Persian eunuch

Lysim- Persian spy

Phytalamus-Rich Persian merchant

Chancony-Phytalamus' son

Mardonis-Persian General- the Kings brother in law

Ho of Sebennytos- Xerxes' Egyptian mother in law.

**Persian Generals**

Tritantaikhmes

Smerdomences

Masistes


Demaratus- Exiled Spartan King, serving Xerxes

Sameron-female lioness- Xerxes Pet

Ahuramazda- Persian God

Del-Marduk-Babylonian God

Tiamat-Internal monster of the human soul

## The Greeks

Themistocles- leader of the Greek Demos

Eudox- Negotiator- Themistocles second in command

Thantos- Adventurer-smuggler-sailor-bound in spirit to Themistocles

Phecontalis-Loyal lieutenant to Thantos

Philokrates-Thespian-leader of Greek delegation to Delphi

Sakarbaal- Phoenician "turncoat"

Leonidas-King of Sparta-17th of the Agiad Line

Gorgo-Leonidas' wife

## Greek Sea Captains

Kallias

Phile

Lasiandra- young Pythia

Aristides "the Just"- exiled Greek politician

## The Players at the Delphic Oracle

Dion- Pythia- Priestess of Oracle

Tryhon- Previous Pythia

Maken-Oracle priest

Akakios- Oracle priest

Demonus-Priest of the Cult of the Soul

Hieronymos- follower of Demonus

Diodotos-messenger to Leonidas

Barick-el-som-Sand Dancer-Assassin

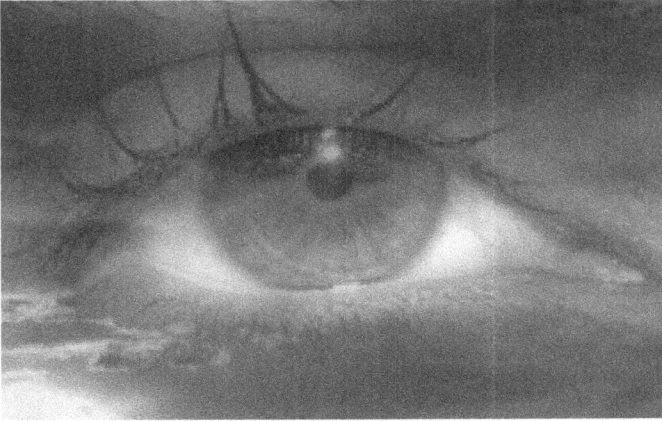

## The Greek Deities

Apollo- God who speak through the Oracle

Dionysus-hedonistic God-Cult of the Soul

Demeter-Goddess- Elysian Mysteries

Athena- Goddess of Athens

Tu-Water Naiad-inhabits the sacred water of Kassotis

Daphne- water nymph

# Preface

At the time in history that this story took place, the Delphic Oracle was already more than a thousand years old. It had influenced Kings and civilizations. The Oracle made prognostations about religion, philosophy, life and death, and history. Men and cultures traveled many days to hear its wisdom.

Delphi was located on the southwest slope of Mount Parnassus. It was told that Zeus had sent two eagles to find the center of the earth, and they met at Delphi. The word, Delphic, is a derivation from the Greek for womb.

The Oracle at Delphi was administered by a religious order made up of priests and vestal priestesses. The priestesses were divided into the Pythias, women who merged with the God Apollo, and younger women who served the Pythias and took care of the barracks. The Pythias was usually chosen from older peasant women who were 'blameless.' The Oracle frequently answered questions in a vague, ethereal fashion. The priests acted as interpreters of the Oracle's prognostations, often recounting the message in hexameters.

There are many Delphic stories, of which I will only mention a few.

Probably the most quoted story is from the great philosopher Socrates. In response to the question from a foreign King: *"who is the smartest man alive?"*, the Oracle responded:

*"Of all men living, Socrates is most wise"*

Upon hearing this conclusion, the great philosopher set out to disprove this conclusion. He was quoted as saying *"what can God mean by this riddle? I know very well that I am not wise! It cannot be that he is speaking falsely, for he is a God, and Gods cannot lie."* After interviewing many of the men that Socrates believed smarter than himself, he concluded:

*"I am wiser than this man. Neither of us knows anything that is really worth knowing, but he thinks that he has knowledge when he has not, while I, having no knowledge, do not think that I have. I seem, at any rate, to be a little wiser than he is on this point I do not think that I know what I do not know."*

On politics, the Oracle said:

Question: "What shall the rulers do to rule well and the citizens to obey?"

Response: *"There are two roads, most distant from each other: the one leading to the honorable house of freedom, the other the house of slavery, which mortals must shun. It is possible to travel the one through manliness and lovely accord; so lead your people to this path. The other they reach through hateful strife and cowardly destruction; so shun it most of all."*

On life and death:

Question. – "Does the soul survive death or does it vanish?"

*Response.* – "While the soul is bound to the body, it yields to mortal ills. But when it finds release at the body's death, it goes entirely to the sky, always ageless, and remains forever whole. For this is the ordinance of divine providence."

And when asked how men can become good, and Godlike, the Oracle said:

"By acting rightly, like the Gods, and telling the truth"

Plutarch, an initiate and careful biographer, explained how the Pythia transmitted the inspiration of Apollo:

"The prophetic priestesses are moved [by the God] each in accordance with her natural faculties... As a matter of fact, the voice is not that of a God, nor the utterance of it, nor the diction, nor the metre, but all these are the woman's; he [Apollo] puts into her mind only the visions, and creates a light in her soul in regard to the future; for inspiration is precisely this. -- *Moralia,* "The Oracles at Delphi," V, 397d

Years in the future, Aristotle would deny the existence of fortune tellers, except of course, for the Delphic Oracle. Plutarch himself, served as one of the priests of the Oracle.

# Preface to Book III

History was quivering as the confluence of opposing forces were all pointing to Delphi in northern Greece. The Persian monarch had a consuming hatred of the Greeks, yet he also seemed to understand the expense and the difficulty of taking such a large army to the Greek peninsula. Why was Xerxes, the King of Kings, even sending a delegation to Delphi? He believed in his own God's omnipotence. Was he attempting a diversion to make the Greeks believe that he was more interested in peace than war? What was his hidden agenda? Did he really want to hear the prognostations of the ancient Oracle? Was it important to him? Would the advice of the God Apollo have any impact on the great Persian King, or was he already hell-bent on the invasion? Would the King of King's alter his strategy if Apollo warned against war? On the Greek side, were they willing to sell out their infantile democracy rather than face the impending invasion and probably genocide? How would Themistocles, the political leader of the Greeks, respond to the Oracle's advice? The Oracle could be blunt in its prognostations. And could the Oracle actually predict how this conflict would play out? As in most areas of history, there were more questions than answers.

But the fact remained that the world was teetering on the brink of the actual first world war. The other historical relevance that was playing out was the first true conflict between absolute oligarcal rule and democracy. How would the course of history be formed by this interplay? What was to come of the governmental experiment of the Demos?

On a more individual level, the Persian empire was ruled by a strong, fit, and aesthetic man, while the Greek Demos was created by what many would call a philanderer and an alcoholic. The Persians, although amalgamated, consisted of many races, many languages and many cultures, all united under one banner, whereas the Greek city states were continually in conflict. Could this Greek politician, Themistocles, unite these disparate cities and philosophies to fight the overwhelming odds that were facing the Greek culture? Most of the Greek cities had already agreed to the Persian King's dominance. Only a small number of Greek cities held firm in their stubborn adherence to their own independence.

The situation was truly desperate.

# Chapter I – Rapture

t was a very dark night, one of those evenings when the moon had disappeared into the abyss. Not a star was obvious in the sky, and the air was heavy with humidity and a gentle fog obscured the area even more. Walking across the path was dangerous because of the absence of any light. The woman walked slowly, almost feeling her way over the path that she knew very well and had trodden on many times. But this night was different, or so it seemed. The woman, well into her thirties, found this walk unnatural, as the fog encompassed many of the well recognizable landmarks on her path. And within this ethereal surrounding, the priestess did not rush. Her legs were heavy and her head was feeling stuffed. Bending over or moving her head too swiftly, brought dizziness and a lightheadedness that was uncomfortable. She feared having to bend for the sensation would increase, leading her closer to falling.

The priestess had traveled this path many times, and she knew that beyond the next bend was a stone bench on which she could rest. Her chest was heavy and her breathing shallow, and even in the eeriness of the surroundings, a short rest would steady her nerves and relax her body. She turned the bend and the vague outline of the bench appeared. The priestess felt the wet grass under her feet as she increased her pace to reach the bench. Her heart was pounding, and her breath unsteady, as she drew closer to the bench. Her neck muscles tightened and she felt an unusual lump within her throat, as she lowered herself onto the cold stone of the resting place. Even though the level of anxiety rose within her stomach, the steadiness of the bench calmed her to a degree.

The priestess looked out over the forest that paralleled the path. There was not much to see as the fog worsened. She could make out the general outline of the trees, but they were covered in a grayish shroud. The priestess sat not knowing how long she would have to wait until returning to her walk. The small building in which she lived was still a distance off from where she rested, and she questioned her ability to continue her journey.

She heard a sound approaching from her left. Someone or something was coming down the path. It was still too far to distinguish who or what it was. The priestess found herself tensing, anticipating the arrival of what was coming toward her. She unsuccessfully tried to settle her thoughts, but her fears seemed to be building out of proportion to what was probably happening.

The priestess was relieved when a figure of a man appeared out of the fog. Before she could identify the figure, his walk was familiar to her. It was the posture and outline of one of the monastery priests. He had a distinguishable gait as he limped towards his right side. Upon this recognition, the priestess seemed to calm, but the lump in her throat remained, as did the pounding of her heart.

The man was closer now, and he began slowing his gait, obviously recognizing her. He approached her place and stood before her. He paused for a moment, then bowed in deference.

*"Good evening, Bion."*

*"Good evening, Maken"*

*"If I may, it is unusual to see you resting during your evening stroll. May I ask if everything is all right?"*

Bion did not immediately answer the inquiry. She stared at the man who stood in front of her for a few heartbeats. Her face was blank, her mouth slightly open, as if she didn't really understand the question. Her eyes closed for a second as she attempted to gather her thoughts. She began to speak. *"Untronce qultabit gentabelnce."*

It was now the priest's turn to stare. The words that she spoke were unknown to him. He had never heard such a language before and he froze, unable to respond to the Pythia who sat before him. He was clearly confused, not knowing to be concerned or troubled by this unrecognizable language. Finally, he found some words of response. *"Pythia, you are making me nervous. Should I help you back to your quarters?"*

Bion continued to stare at the man. Her head seemed to bend forward as her eyes closed for a second. She wanted to sleep but resisted the urge. Again, a blank stare appeared on her face, as if she was seeing past Maken. Her throat was beating and her head was becoming heavier. Bion reached for her head and began massaging her sinuses. Again she uttered, *"Maken, I am fine. You don't need to feel concerned. I am just feeling the heaviness of the fog"*

The priest bowed again, still obviously concerned. But, even though alarmed, Maken began backing away. He stared again at her, then continued on his walk. But his stride was slower and he looked back at the Pythia at least twice as he disappeared into the fog.

Bion watched Maken slowly disappear into the mist. Her mind was empty as she felt the heaviness return to her temples. She decided that she had to continue her walk, but strangely, she felt the need to go to the Temple rather than return to her room. It was not a far walk from her bench and Bion veered away from the path, taking a shortcut through the woods. As she walked, she grabbed onto some of the trees to keep her balance. She was still very unsteady. As she came closer to the Temple of Apollo, her thoughts seemed to disperse, focusing only on her desire to reach the Temple.

At this time of night, the Temple was usually unguarded. The Pythia moved through the chambers until she reached the famous tripod on which she merged with the God Apollo. She now stood transfixed, staring at the tripod with a far distant gaze. Her mind was now completely blank, and she stood mesmerized by the inner sanctum. None of the candles were lit, but the room was surprisingly bright. And then, without warning, a blue light appeared and seemed to engulf the tripod. She found herself drawn to this pastel colored apparition. The light then began drifting, growing in volume and slowly moving toward where she stood. She was rooted to the spot, unable to move. Bion's chest was now on fire with a pain that passed through her being. Although feeling faint, the Pythia stood rigidly in her place, unable to move her limbs. She felt like falling, lying down on the ground, closing her eyes, but she stood still.

The blue vapor now engulfed the Pythia, and she began seizing while she stood. She had now lost all voluntary muscular control, and she hung suspended by this bluish cloud. The pain in her chest had stopped, her heart was now stable, but she had also lost conscious control of her body. Bion was not scared at this unusual state of events. She was relatively calm.

As she seemed to float slightly above the ground, she noticed that her body was absorbing the blue aura. It seemed to be infusing itself within her limbs and torso. An image was appearing in front of her eyes. It was unclear, vague.

The horses were tired and sweaty. There were opportunities to change horses along the Royal Road. Built by Xerxes' father, Darius the Great, the road stretched 1677 miles from Susa to Sardis, from the desert to the sea. It would take riders seven days to transverse the great road. Every fifty miles or so, there were established way stations used to exchange for fresh horses, and provide some sustenance for the riders. But unfortunately there were some stations were no fresh animals existed, or there were not enough animals for the entire entourage. It was because of this that the animals that were not replaced until the following station struggled mightily as the miles passed. In addition to this practical inconvenience, the weather had not cooperated. It had been hot and very dry, and the mouths of the group tasted like the desert wasteland itself. Five horses had already died on this journey and had been left for the crows, along with some slaves who could not be supported. The group finally had passed the satrap of Phrygia and was headed to the sea town of Phocaea on the Lydian coast. From there the group was scheduled to meet the Phoenician ship, the Phoinikes, to cross the Aegean Sea.

The journey to the Greek mainland across the dangerous Aegean was a precarious two hundred and fifty mile journey. The Aegean was known for its changing hazardous currents and sudden hurricane like storms. Many ships had already tasted the depths of the Aegean because of its abruptly appearing and furious storms.

As the entourage drew closer to the Aegean, the demeanor of Warrior Queen of Halicarnassus seemed to lineally improve. Artemisia was not a desert princess. She was the Queen of the water. Like a fish returning to its spawning grounds, the Warrior Queen sought the beauty and recognizable comfort of the open sea. She was drawn to it, and she had to answer its call. There was a magnetic pull which increased in intensity as she approached. It was an invisible yearning but a powerful source nonetheless. Artemisia herself was a capricious lover, but her true adoration, her burning desire, was for the open water.

Twenty miles before reaching the ocean, she claimed that she could begin to smell the salt water. Her fellow travelers laughed at this delusional folly, as the ocean was still miles away when she made the claim. But Artemisia was serious in her proclamation, and she did not respond positively to the laughing by the others. The Warrior Queen had a trigger temper. Her boiling point was quickly reached, especially by those she considered irrelevant to her own needs. It was rumored that the Warrior Queen once threw a temper in which fifteen others lost their lives. She had no fear of others, nor worry for repercussions from her actions. She was bold in her responses and tenacious in her desire. Artemisia did not allow comments to, 'role off her back.' Instead, they stuck in her side and she was sadistically revengeful. In a male dominated world, the Queen of Halicarnassus was the exception to the rule. She was, and considered herself, the Alpha. Even to the dominance of the great Xerxes, The King of Kings, she only reluctantly bowed.

The journey from Susa along the hot and desert like Royal Road, had been interpersonally contentious. The members of this entourage all had forceful, dominant personalities. Although each respected the reputations of the other members, none of the individuals had spent extensive time together. It was ironic that each member's admiration for the talents of the others never generalized to deference. Each person in the delegation was accomplished in their own right, and each possessed strong egos. They were all used to having others listen to their views and bow to their wishes. There were very few people in the civilized world that these eminent people had to listen to. Although the King of Kings appointed all the members of this caravan, he purposely left it leaderless. He didn't want any of these people whom he respected to feel jilted and undervalued. So he equalized them, leaving them leaderless. Therefore, this unusual combination of people, all accomplished and having the largest egos in the empire, traveled the Royal Road with only themselves, the horses, the sand, and the bugs as associates.

Bored and sore from the long endless ride, the travelers became testy and often irritable. This led to both conflict and heated discussion, the experienced warriors in the group jockeyed for dominance. A few times others feared that this interpersonal rivalry would lead to physical confrontation. But, although close at times, cooler heads always eventually prevailed.

Artemisia, the famous Warrior Queen, started the journey as a distant debutant. Her jaw remained clenched for the first week of the journey. She neither spoke with, nor looked directly at, any of the other members. She always sat very high in the saddle, refusing to ride on the accompanying wagons. Her reputation as a fearless, aggressive antagonist, did not apply to cavalry fighting. In fact, she disliked the horse, felt that it had an unpleasant odor. She had learned to ride as a young child, but never really took to it. As she grew, her love of the ocean geometrically grew as fast as her dislike of the horse. More than that, her reputation as a superior sailor rivaled that of her 'brothers', the Phoenicians. In the known world, the Phoenicians were considered the greatest navigators that had ever lived. Artemisia had grown up with the Phoenicians and neither considered the other as outsiders. The Phoenicians treated Artemisia as royalty. She knew both their spoken and unspoken language. They were very protective of this unusual woman. Her sailing skills rivaled, and in battle exceeded, their own. Considering that the Phoenicians were considered the world's most accomplished sailors, and they considered Artemisia more skilled then they were, it was truly great praise indeed.

With Artemisia on this expedition were five of those fierce Phoenician warriors. They were hard men, all of whom had bodies covered with scars of battles. As quiet and distant as Artemisia acted, the Phoenicians made her appear excitable. They were also stoic and without overt emotion. These guards were on duty all the time. Their lives were devoted to protecting their charge, for they considered her the equal of their Kings. The oldest of these bodyguards had known Artemisia since she was a young adolescent. He was a tall, quiet man, whose stare reminded one of a stalking lion, focused and unrelenting. He seemed to stare through people as his lower lip would turn down. If asked a question by anyone other than the Queen, he would just turn his head and walk the other way. He was protective, and usually kept within sight of the Queen. He had used all of his influence with King Matten to be assigned to protecting Artemisia on this journey to Greece. His name was Adon, and the honors he had received from his King were widely known. Adon had been one of the leaders of the Phoenician colony of Carthage, but he bored quickly of administration.

Like the Persian monarch, Adon also hated the Greeks. While in Carthage, he was a stern administrator, establishing and ruthlessly enforcing the rule of law. When upset or disgusted with someone's behavior, Adon would grunt and turn his head. He remained aloof and detached from all non-Phoenicians. Adon mostly spoke without words. Only other Phoenicians were learned in this unspoken language. This communication consisted mostly of hand signs and gestures. The Phoenicians would touch parts of their body to relay their wishes. How hard, how quick a touch occurred, meant different messages. Raising your hand to one of your body parts conveyed your feelings about whatever discussion was occurring. It was specific and unrecognizable to others, as the subtlety of movement meant everything.

On the opposite end of the spectrum, in terms of temperament from the Warrior Queen was Hamas, nicknamed, 'the teacher,' by the King of Kings. His successes on the battlefield were

legendary, as his victories over many races left his name cursed
in many cultures. Hamas was one of the few military leaders who
was able to strategize both offensively and defensively when the
situation warranted it. Hamas rarely made the same military
mistake twice. He was one of the few military people who argued
against taking the army to Greece. Hamas didn't believe that you
should fight the same war twice. Although he wasn't at Marathon,
the Persian defeat still stuck in his throat, but he believed he could
spit out his hatred in favor of rationality. Hamas believed that by
going back to Greece, Xerxes was fighting his father's war. It was
Darius the Great who was embarrassed at Marathon, not his son,
Xerxes. Hamas didn't believe in fighting memories. It was his
opinion that his King was making the same mistake his father did
by re-attacking Attica. The Empire was large enough, and
keeping all the various peoples in line was a difficult task. He
advised the King of Kings to erase the memory of Marathon, to
not purposely keep it burning, like the young King had decided.
There were few who held the King's ear, and even fewer who
could suggest such a drastic detour from the expected and live.
Besides his military skill, Hamas was a master swordsman. It was
said he could not be bested in a sword fight. He had worked hours
with the young Xerxes, teaching him inner discipline, the one-
mindedness of swordsmanship.

Hamas was a general who always kept his composure under
pressure. In fact he believed an army should create chaos in the
opponent, while also making the enemy think that his own troops
and strategic position were in disorder. Hamas would lure the
enemy into making mistakes by baiting them into overconfidence.
He was an expert in spreading false rumors about positions of
troops and using enemy spies in order to tempt his adversary into
attacking his defensive strengths. Hamas didn't want the enemy
to understand his line of attack. He was not vain in believing in

the omnipotence of his troops. One of Hamas' favorite offensive strategies was to divide and conquer. If he wanted to control the left flank, he would first attack the right, baiting and hoping to deceive his enemy. Many of his strategies depended on trickery. He preached to the young King that it was not the largest army that won battles, but the army that was most prepared. Their generals had to be men of foresight, not just men of birth. Hamas taught the young King that dealing with people and governments was akin to fishing in cloudy waters. You had to outsmart the fish, without being able to see them.

Artemisia's approach to war was diametrically different to that of Hamas, both in theory and practice. She wanted to destroy the enemy. She was single minded and merciless. She was bold to the point of audacity. Unlike Hamas, who believed in strategic deception, Artemisia believed in provoking the enemy. Hamas spoke of the importance of fear in the general's mind. It helped him to separate his beliefs from his wishes. Artemisia did not believe in fear. She did not accept its existence in her army. She felt that fear was contagious, worse than any disease, and if you could plant it in your opponent it would drain the enemy's heart. Artemisia wanted to create the most treacherous and bloody reputation that she could, to spread fear even before the attack began. The enemy would want to retreat before the battle began. She was seen as unpredictable, daring, and aggressively foolish at times. The Warrior Queen believed in striking first and striking hard. She wanted to be seen as relentless. She wanted people to shake when hearing her name. She was antagonistic to the extreme, and took no quarter.

Hamas and Artemisia were an unlikely duo for this mission. Their discussions themselves were warfare disguised. During one evening their conversation almost came to blows, instigated of course by the Warrior Queen. She baited the teacher with continuing sarcasm. It was difficult to bluff this woman, because with every move you made, she became more belligerent. It was only Hamas' fine-tuned internal discipline that held him from being provoked by the constant disdain. At times, her comments were just short of mockery. Hamas figured that the best approach with her was to avoid her. He would not allow her words to strike him. But, like a hungry hyena, Artemisia was relentless in pursuit, especially when she smelled blood.

One evening, when the camp was quiet, Artemisia approached Hamas who was sitting around his camp fire and talking with some of the guards. She slowly sat and was quiet for a few minutes. But suddenly she turned to Hamas and in an apparently genuine fashion asked, *"So, my ally, what are your thoughts about the great King's desire to conquer Greece?"*

Hamas smiled at the inquiry, then responded, *"My King is more knowledgeable than I am. If he tells me to take the army to Greece, all the generals will comply and the army will march."*

The Queen seemed irritated at the response, but gathered herself, controlling her temper for the time. She lowered her head and took a deep breath. Her face seemed to soften as she turned to the teacher. *"You will forgive my insolence, general. I am a sea child and horses make me uncomfortable and irritable. I know I have provoked you and I apologize for any annoyance that I caused. I am restless and I can smell the ocean. I am becoming agitated at the prospect."* She paused and allowed Hamas to consider her words. She then continued *"Hamas, we both hope to support our monarch. You will control the land and I and my brothers will control the sea."*

Hamas looked sideways at Artemisia with this comment, for the prevailing belief in the great empire, was that the God, Ahura Mazda, favored large ground forces. Hamas had little military use for the navy. When this entourage eventually reached the sea, it would be the first sea voyage for the teacher. He was not looking forward to the experience. He believed the sea was a deadly place. It engulfed many sailors, with horrible winds and storms arriving with no warning. It was not a part of war and conflict that Hamas understood. Hamas' fear went so deep that his dreams were engulfed with thoughts of large waves and sinking vessels. He would wake with terrible gastrointestinal issues and numbness in his arms and fingers. The dreams were so realistic, that he could almost taste the saltiness of the water in his mouth. At one point, Hamas seemed to tremble after waking. Artemisia looked at him, smiled to herself, looked at one of the slaves, pointed at the teacher and said, *"Thalassa!" (the Greek word for the ocean).* Even with his internal discipline, it was easy to read the confusion on Hamas' face at this sudden change in attitude from Artemisia. To trust this metamorphosis would be foolish, and the teacher found himself listening to her words with a skeptical mind. The Warrior Queen went on, *"Hamas, I must admit to you that I was angry about being chosen to make this trip. I am not a diplomat, I am not much of a talker. I am more a doer."*

The eyebrows of the teacher rose slightly at the obvious admission. The Warrior Queen then turned to face the general. With a sardonic reference to the great Oracle, she said, *"I have no use for fortune tellers from false Gods. I don't believe our King believes in this nonsense. So I don't really understand why we are making this journey".*

She now rose slowly from her seated position. *"I am having trouble sitting still, especially riding that stinking animal."* She looked at the teacher and smiled. *"You must admit that these animals blowing their smell out of their asses and the constant shit dropping without warning is irritating."*

Again she smiled, but quickly became more serious. *"You know, I love Xerxes, and I will follow him to Hades if he asked me to, but why ask me waste my time with this folly?"*

She paused, as if in thought. She then clarified, *"I will follow Xerxes to hell as long as he lets me fight. I will not negotiate with undergods."*

Hamas straightened himself, ignored the last comment and asked, *"Do you not believe the power of this Oracle?"*

Before thinking, and with a scowl on her face, Artemisia sarcastically asked, *"Do you?"*

Hamas thought, but then said, *"I believe what the great Xerxes tells me to believe. If he sees value in this Oracle, then it must have worth."*

*"I always respected you, Hamas, but now I hear that you don't think"*

She looked more aggressively at him now. Her forehead wrinkled and her posture bent forward. She continued, *"Tell me the truth. Do not preach blind faith to me. We are both warriors. I know you have your own thoughts and do not blindly follow foolishness."*

The Queen settled her irritation. She then took a breath and said, *"Hamas, if we are to be allies, then I need to know how you really feel. The great King is not here. I need to know your heart. Don't tell me rubbish."*

When Hamas responded his face took on a strange expression. *"Artemisia, I have heard of your reputation. I would much rather have you as an ally than as an adversary. If we find ourselves in a military situation I will treat you like my sister. But I will not engage in a philosophical argument about the great King. We are not discussing the great King, Hamas. We are talking about the Oracle at Delphi. I don't wish to argue about the King"*

Hamas rose and slowly walked to the Queen. He did not respond to her last comment. When he reached her, the teacher slowly bowed in deference to the woman. It was an unusual gesture, and Artemisia stood rigidly, not knowing how to respond to this movement. Hamas rose and slowly walked to his tent, leaving the Warrior Queen staring in disbelief. *"He is a fool,"* the Queen thought, as she watched him go.

*"I thought of him a great warrior, but he follows the child King blindly. No general should sell his soul to inept leadership!"*

The Queen silently spit on the ground and walked away. Her attempt at reconciliation was an awkward failure.

The buildings formed a square around a beautifully tended garden. Two separate streams fed the garden and both formed small waterfalls that highlighted the center of the area. There were many benches made of fine sandalwood, interspersed among the stone paths that snaked through this large area. The flower beds were meticulously manicured, and the colors that surrounded the paths made one want to stop and meditate, cleansing the mind of the pollution of the day. At the edges of this conclave stood two large trees that hovered over about a third of the garden. In their shade, the flowers were less spectacular, but the ambiance of the area was enhanced by their shade.

One of the two small, horizontal waterfalls was more aggressive than its more placid sister. At any time during the day, there were numerous gardeners tending and shaping the bushes, gracefully carving the flowers and branches. It was a delicate art, and they competed with each other for the admiration and approval of the priestesses. These religious women were usually distracted by their own thoughts and purposely appeared not to notice the devotion that the gardeners put into their craft. The priestesses tended to wander through the garden, at times sitting for hours in their trance. They were distant people, seemingly lost in their own ponderings. They seemed to float through the garden proper, but each had their favorite spot and would often return to that area.

There were 15 priestesses in the compound and ten male priests. Each gender group had their own complex and the two groups had only brief contact, as their prescribed tasks kept them separate. The priests spent their lifetimes in service to this site. Part of their job was to greet the congregants and the pilgrims who came from very long distances. But the primary jobs of the priests were to interpret the mystifying responses of the Pythia.

The Pythia was a mystical creature. In fact, there were three reigning Pythias, each taking turns communicating with the God, Apollo. But in essence, there was one Pythia that led the other two.

The God communicated with the pilgrims through the Pythia. She was the chalice through which the voice of the God flowed. Apollo's message was often subtle and perplexing. He sometimes spoke in multifarious rhymes and understated poems. It was these concealed and oblique messages that the priests would recount and help interpret for the pilgrims. Sometimes the God was clear and direct, whereas at other times, the messages were imperceptive and presented in complex riddles. But as subtle and delicate the messages from Apollo were, the joining of the God with the Pythia was anything but insubstantial. The Pythias often shuddered at this rapture in great distress, screaming and holding their breasts as if they were being ripped from their bodies. They would sweat and seize, sometimes screaming in ancient languages that no one could understand. Their voices took on a low, ominous tone, and they salivated from their mouths and eyes as they spoke. Their eyes fell back into their sockets and their voices sounded extra-terrestrial. Possessed by any deity was a frightening and life threatening procedure. Pythias had died during the rapture. It was told that one Pythia turned blue during rapture, and she began coughing so hard that organs from her stomach appeared in her mouth.

There were three women who achieved the rank of Pythia. The triad achieved this exalted status after years of devotion, sacrifice, and spiritual growth. To reach this level, a priestess had to endure years of trials. But commitment was the least of the qualities that was required for ascension and rapture with the God. A woman considered to achieve the level of Pythia had to be able to touch the past and predict the future. Before becoming Pythia, the woman's skills and sensitivities had to be proven. There was a tribunal of senior priestesses that either confirmed the woman's achievement as "lacosiant" or miraculous. The Pythia was, after all, the vassal that reached into the future, transcended the gap between man and deity, and fused in mind and spirit with the God.

The three Pythia took turns in communicating with Apollo, as the task was so physically draining, and at times so life threatening, that it was very dangerous for one to assume the lone responsibility for the merger. Throughout their history, a number of women reached such a direct level of communication with the God, and, in the end, their lives on earth were forfeited to the symbiosis. The life of the Pythia was short-lived, either succumbing to the God-connection or strangely losing the power of telepathy and visionary ability. The three Pythia had varying ability, and the Pythia which joined the God for specific pilgrims often depended on the stature of the people asking the question of Apollo.

At the current time, the most senior, and also the most spiritually perceptive of the three was named Bion. Many of the priestesses in the cult of the Oracle mystics came from local villages. But Bion was from a faraway place. Her ascension to the position of principal Pythia was outstanding and unheard of considering her alien origins. Every year, five or more woman entered the complex as acolytes. They were all circumcised and within the first three months, the majority of the young initiates had already left or were cast out. It was not unusual for only one of the initial number to survive the first year. Initiation into the mystical cult happened only after two years of living within the priestly complex and passing many initiation rituals. Many signs had to be read by the elder women, positively foretelling the potential of greatness that the initiate possessed. There were many ways to read the signs from the God, from the faint whistling of certain trees to the flight patterns of sacred eagles. After all, these great birds were released by the almightily Zeus to find the center of the earth. They ended up settling at Delphi, proclaiming the holiness and centricity of this area. As the millenniums passed, the eagles, gained spiritual importance. There were many sub-cults across the land devoted entirely to this mystical reading of their shrieking and flying patterns.

From the moment that Bion arrived at the complex, it was obvious to the elders that her innate abilities were far superior to those of any of the other initiates, and already rivaled that of the sitting Pythias. She required no training as she was innately able to acquire power from beyond the human existence. Bion was initially given the job of cleansing and blessing the tripod on which the Pythia sat. One evening, without the knowledge of anyone else, she stealthily went down and inhaled the revered mist. Other priestesses discovered the child missing and hearing screams, rushed to her side in the caves below the temple proper. What they found was most disturbing, even for them. Bion was slinking along the ground like a great cobra. She finally rose and spit blood on those watching. In horror, the other priestesses bowed and fell to their knees. Bion fell on her back and began shaking uncontrollably. She then began speaking in a language that sounded Semitic, but was unrecognizable to those around her. After a few minutes, as the other priestesses looked in astonishment, her arms began to glow as if she was being consumed by fire from within. This first unauthorized rapture almost cost her existence. And most surprisingly, Bion was only 14 when she entered the cult of the mystics and had this visionary experience. Because of her extraordinary abilities, she immediately became a prophete, or one of the assistants to the principal Pythia, who, at the time, was named Tryhon. Four years after Bion's arrival into the cult, Tryhon died after an unusually potent rapture with Apollo. Bion was there at the time that Tryhon began her journey through the underworld.

Much to the chagrin of some of the other priestesses, Tryhon had taken Bion under her wing almost immediately after she arrived. Over the years she schooled her in the intricate rituals that the Pythia would have to follow on the seventh of every month that Apollo was at Delphi. She also taught her the secrets of dealing with the Naiads. Every sacred stream and river in Greece was occupied and protected by these mysterious water nymphs. The Kassotis were the sacred waters that lay under Delphi and Apollo's temple. The Pythia had to bath in this hallowed stream before attempting rapture with the God. But to co-opt the naiads was a daunting task. This was only a small part of the elaborate preparatory sacrament that led to eventual bliss. These surreptitious rites were hidden from most of the priestesses and the priests, as only a select few were initiated into their secrets. That they were being shared with a mere child who had not originated from Delphi and hadn't proven her worth made Bion many enemies within the order. But even though others ruminated in jealously, they also feared Bion's obvious power and gifts. So she also acquired many false friends.

Tryhon schooled the young acolyte as meticulously as she had been taught. She admitted one night that she had foreseen Bion's emergence as one of the great Pythias. But an ominous warning followed this precocious prediction.

*"Bion, the premonition I had last night involved your future. It foretold both your ascension and your demise. You will be a truly profound Pythia, but you will pay the ultimate price for allowing the spirit of the God to enter your body before Apollo is ready. If you decide to accept the role as Pythia, much danger awaits. My vision revealed that your death would not be from rapture, but from an outside source."*

Bion looked in surprise at her mentor. Her face beckoned the question. But before she could speak any words, Tryhon spoke again, *"No, no, my child. I cannot see the event clearly. It is vague and shrouded in mist. Do not fear it child, for it is already written. Your path is laid and you must follow it to the conclusion."*

The experience of rapture that signaled the beginning of the eventual demise of Tryhon's worldly existence ended with the Pythia seizing in cascading waves of convulsions. Her eyes appeared to disappear into her skull and a frothy liquid oozed from her mouth. The experience lasted almost two hours, then ended as quickly as it began. Bion had stayed by the Pythia's side through the experience, and when she seemed to be drifting into the void, Tryhon called Bion to her side. Bion held her hand, which was already becoming clammy. With a tremendous expenditure of energy, Tryhon pulled the young Bion close to her and quietly spoke in her ear. *"My young Bion. You will be Pythia soon, as I am beginning on my journey into infinity. Rapture with the God Apollo is beyond anything you can imagine. Your experience did not truly represent its beauty. No voice carries further, no authority can overrule it, no might is more powerful, and no seer has better sight. You will hear the will of the God, although no voice will be evident to you. You will feel his company, but his presence will not be obvious. He will overtake your body, but you will not feel him enter. The God will massage your body and impregnate your mind with his thoughts. You will think and experience things you never have before. You will feel him touch your skin and control your subsistence. If you choose to remain in the cult, you must learn to extinguish your thoughts in favor of the God's will. Do you understand these things, Bion?"*

*I do, mistress!*

Tryhon closed her eyes and then reopened them. *"Bion, you will die from the affliction of becoming Pythia, as I have. I have already foretold you of this occurrence. But the rapture, Bion, the rapture is greater than any feeling that your body could imagine. The spirit will enter your body, and you will speak in different languages that have become extinct eons ago. But in its ecstasy comes a price, and that cost is a premature earthly death. Every rapture brings you closer to the God and closer to eternal infinity. You will forever become one with the God. Do not fear the end, my dear. You will not walk it alone. I will clear the path and we will walk together through time immortal."*

She then smiled, squeezed Bion's hand, and closed her eyes for the final time.

The loss of her friend and mentor was overwhelming for the young priestess. She had never before experienced such a burning loss. Life without Tryhon was impossible to comprehend, and yet she knew that it had to be. After two days of tears, Bion had a vision that death was stalking her. She stared at this visionary monster coming slightly closer every day. But every time she caught it gazing at her, she smiled and gazed back.

The God, Apollo, spent nine months in Delphi. In the three months that Apollo ventured away from his temple, the temple was taken over by his brother, Dionysus. In the three months away from Delphi, Apollo visited his other temples at Corinth, Bassae, Delos, and Aegina. He made no human contact at the other temples, but enjoyed the reverence that was shown him by the worshipers.

Dionysus was Apollo's alter ego. As Apollo represented order and rationality, Dionysus was the lord of hedonistic pleasure. In the three months of Apollo's absence, Dionysus ruled from a cave seven miles north of the temple. During this time of chaos, later to be called winter, the Pythia, her priestesses and the priests of the temple hibernated in their complex. They spent the three months praying and fasting, hoping that Apollo returned to vanquish his brother and reestablish order. When Dionysus took over the temple, the season of death ruled at Delphi. Rebirth would occur when Apollo returned to subjugate his younger brother.

As Demeter had the cult of contemplation, teaching her followers the Elysian Mysteries, Dionysus initiated young people every year into the Dionysian Cult of the Soul. The Elysian Mysteries taught meditation leading to reflection and insight. The Dionysian Cult of the Soul was based on organismic pleasure, physical pain, and death. Insight, for Dionysus, was based on the satisfying of carnal need and desire. In the three months of drunken debauchery when Dionysus ruled Delphi, there were some deaths and frequent beatings, as well as masochistic and sadistic rituals. Human blood offerings were one of the central themes of the Dionysian cult of the soul. It was believed that human blood infused the God's spirit into the initiate. It was said that rapture with the God, Dionysus, occurred only during drunken orgasm.

As far back as his memory went, Hieronymos worshipped Dionysus. Now that he turned 15 he was eligible to become a male initiate into the Cult of the Soul. His father and family had warned the young Hieronymos of the dangers of going to Delphi. Not fazed by the admonition, Hieronymos disappeared one morning embarking on his portentous journey. He had none of the fears that his father held. He secretly considered his father to be an alarmist. In his heart, Hieronymos knew that he belonged in the heart of Dionysus' breast. Hieronymos had been praying to Dionysus since he was a child. Much to his father's dislike, Hieronymos was proud of his affiliation with the orgasmic God. Whereas other deities were paid homage to during the daylight hours, Dionysus was worshiped after the sun went to sleep for the night.

Unlike other young men of his age, Hieronymos showed no inclination to be attracted to woman. There were rumors about his sexual preference, some gossip even suggesting that Hieronymos preferred inanimate objects for his carnal pleasure. By temperament he was a quiet, reserved young man, not taken to argument. His nature was placid and docile. When Hieronymos became devoted to the God, his dress changed to match the popular concept about the nature of Dionysus. He let his curly hair grow long, and he began applying heavy makeup to his face. A delicate and almost frail looking young man, Hieronymos was never really able to find friends, and he spent most of his free time admiring his features. He combed and re-combed his hair trying different styles to satisfy his taste. Many hours were spent experimenting with different colored makeup to highlight his eyes and his thin jaw and neck.

Feeling as an outcast, Hieronymos believed that he had no future staying home. It was a place where he felt both alienated and unwanted. Hieronymos lived in a small village that was on the island of Zakynthos, north west of Sparta and in the Mediterranean Sea. Although not part of Sparta per se, the island had a strong and long Spartan influence. Spartan philosophy only made Hieronymos' life more difficult. An effeminate young man of Hieronymos' frail stature would most likely be castrated and turned into a house slave. He believed his only choice was to flee and follow his true destiny.

Although he planned to reach Delphi to join the cult, he hadn't planned how to get there. He realized this fact within the first day of leaving his home. In his frustration, Hieronymos eventually prostituted himself, negotiating a ride for his service on a commercial caravan traveling to Athens. To his surprise he enjoyed the sexual experience, looking forward to some of the older men in the caravan visiting his tent at night. Hieronymos found he became aroused imagining their hairy chests and legs. It was a satisfying, but not totally surprising awakening for the young man.

When he arrived in Delphi, Hieronymos was drained from his arduous journey. But even though emotionally and physically exhausted, he was as convinced as ever that he belonged with the God, Dionysus, in the Cult of the Soul. Hieronymos spent a few days in the town of Delphi and was directed to the cave in which the priestly rituals were held. Once arriving there he was met by a Dionysian priest. The man's name was Demonus and he looked at Hieronymos in a questioning manner.

Demonus was an odd looking man. He had a long beard, but it was unkempt and one could imagine that it hadn't been washed in many moons. His face was wrinkled and his eyebrows were quite large and bushy, covering what appeared to be the top half of his head. The hairs sprung out in all directions. He also had copious amounts of hair protruding from his ears. The appearance of this man set Hieronymos back and he gasped at the sight. The priest looked him up and down and spoke to him, *"You look young, my fellow. Why have you come here?"*

Hieronymos averted his eyes, not really knowing how to answer the priest. He expected to be welcomed without question. It took a number of heartbeats until he looked back up. Finally, he tried to straighten his back, swallowed hard, and said: *"Sir, I am a devote of the God, Dionysus. I have come here to join the*

*Cult of the Soul. I have journeyed far with some distress to arrive here. Will you offer me a place to rest?"*

The priest looked through the young man as if his questions were irritating and taking up his precious time. *"Well, I suppose we can find room for an urchin."* He then leaned forward and asked in a menacing tone, *"But tell me, young man, do you like pain?"* Hieronymos just stared in fright at the older man. Demonus stared at him for a few minutes with saliva dripping from his mouth. He stared again at the young man's body then laughed. The priest turned and led the lost young man to austere quarters in the back of an area that housed horses.

His ass and back were revolting against him. For all the miles between Athens and Delphi, the pain seemed to worsen with every foot, every inch. He cursed the road, cursed the Gods, and most of all, cursed Themistocles. He had followed that man in every adventure he had conceived, no matter how unlikely the odds of success were. He agreed with Themistocles' philosophical view of man, his religious view of the Gods, and his pragmatic view of politics and government. Many years ago Eudox knew that he was a slave to his friend. Up until now, Themistocles had appeared mystical and almost clairvoyant. He had the Métis, that extraordinary God given ability to understand and foretell events. It was rumored that the Goddess, Athena herself, gave Themistocles this supernatural capacity. Many times Eudox wondered at the ways that Themistocles dodged failure. He seemed to anticipate trouble and react before tragedy set in. From the assassination attempts, to the political attempts to destroy the Demos, he was politically indomitable. But even with all his successes, Eudox wondered when the man would make a mistake. When would the odds finally catch up with him. And Eudox knew that when fate caught up with Themistocles, the penalty would simultaneously catch up with him as well. Themistocles was self-confident, bordering on delusional, and this worried the loyal Eudox. Themistocles could charm those whom he needed for support. But as sophisticated as his political facility was, it was only rivaled by his drunkenness and debauchery. Eudox never understood the dichotomy. How could a man with such insight, and the ability to peer into the face of uncertainty, fall into the depth of inebriated unconsciousness? Eudox would find him lying head first in his own vomit. The next day, following such addictive withdrawal, Themistocles would perform the most unusual political gymnastics. Eudox was a consistent political activist. Variation of mood and approach was an unusual occurrence for him. And yet he was tied to a man whose political activities were more reminiscent of a changing weather pattern, a storm arriving from the west.

As he rode in the cart on his trip to Delphi, Eudox recalled the day he met his mentor. Eudox was an experienced politician when he walked through the bazaar looking to buy lunch. There was a disturbance and Eudox was surprised by the chaos, flinching as he turned to look at the commotion. As he did, he tripped over a log that was lying on the ground by his feet. Eudox fell flat on his face, cutting his lip with his teeth. As he lay on the ground feeling self-conscious over his clumsiness, a hand reached down to help him. As Eudox looked up at the man smiling down at him, he could feel something. It was electric, and Eudox lost consciousness for a split second. It was almost as if he lost himself for a heartbeat, having gone to a faraway place. It scared him more than the fall did. He then heard a voice.

*"Are you all right, my fellow?"*

THE DELPHIC ORACLE · 41

Eudox grunted in return, seemingly transfixed as he stared into the eyes of this stranger. That's when it started. He was mesmerized from the beginning. But how could such a brilliant mind bend to the basal needs of overindulgence? Eudox thought.

It was confusing to him as the parts of the Themistocles' puzzle didn't seem to fit. When sober, he was the most imaginable genius, yet when drunk not even mice could match his wretchedness. He was a very popular man. Themistocles appealed to all, and because of a superior memory, seemed to remember everyone in context of their own life. He loved to gamble, and there were always rumors that Themistocles was anticipating monetary gain from any conflict with Persia. Eudox even heard that people believed that the Persian monarch was paying Themistocles, and that he was secretly planning the fall of the Greek culture. His debauchery with woman was infamous, and he would frequent whore houses and drink the cheapest of wines till reaching oblivion.

As the cart bounced along the rocky road, Eudox mused about all the quests that were undertaken in the name of the great Themistocles. His mind drifted miles away from the cart, as the wheels bounced over the gravelly road. As his mind wandered, his thoughts drifted away from the pain in his body, giving his limbs and bones some desperately needed relief. He looked over at his traveling companions and wondered if this group had any chance of succeeding at Delphi. What was more confusing was that he didn't really understand what success meant. This oracle scared him. It wasn't logical; in fact he was skeptical about all mystics and spiritualists. He found in his experience that mystics have 'revelations' that tended to favor their own fortunes and hidden agendas. It left him cynical and doubting of all fortune tellers, no less than this Oracle that claimed to receive information from Apollo himself. And yet here he was, traveling with this odd group, going to the greatest soothsayer of the day, the Oracle at Delphi. His back and thighs hurt just thinking of this journey.

Eudox had known many mystics, many of whom were obvious frauds. But this Oracle had been around for at least a thousand years, and its predictions were deadly accurate. He couldn't clear his doubts and accept that this was not some fraud trying to make a name for itself or attempting to gain favor with some unknown emperor. The Pythia, or so these priestesses were called, actually had had both physical and divine contact with the God Apollo. It was called rapture, this earthly and deatic union, an experience in which the woman was infused with Apollo's essence, allowing her a window to the future, and a direct view of the God's thoughts.

*"Was this even possible?"*

The steadfast logician that Eudox was continued to ponder. It didn't fit any deductive pattern that he knew he did. The difficulty with this logic was that his assumption was that the Oracle was a fraud. But how could it be? Was it just guessing? It couldn't be guessing for the success rate was too high. So if it wasn't guessing, if it was actually seeing the truth, then the Pythia must actually be rapturing with the God. Eudox had investigated the predictions of the Oracle and found it was remarkable in its accuracy.

It gave Eudox chills to wonder whether this great Oracle knew of the outcome of the impending power struggle between the great Persian King and the budding Greek Demos. The future of this great political experiment that he and Themistocles sponsored hinged on the Pythia and the God Apollo. But, he wondered, how could Apollo side with the King of Kings over the Greek Demos? But what if he did? What if Apollo wanted to punish the Athenians for their devotion to the Goddess Athena or worse, harbor anger at the Greeks for turning away from the Gods in favor of the reason of their own thoughts? It frightened Eudox to think that their reason and logic would be the basis for which their destruction was based.

But Eudox' thoughts eventually roamed to an even more puzzling area. Even though he had spoken with Themistocles in depth about this mission, he still wasn't sure how to define success. Even though he knew Themistocles better than almost anyone alive, he had difficulty determining what his expectations were. He completely misread his mentor's desires when he traveled to speak with the ugly dictator of Syracuse.

Eudox' understanding of the mission changed a few times after having listened to his mentor speak. Themistocles was vague and evasive, an unusual characteristic for him. It was as if he himself didn't understand the best purpose of this assignment. Through their two-day discussion, Eudox sometimes thought that Themistocles wanted to seek a settlement with the Persians, giving in to a number of demands in favor of saving the Demos. Then, at other times, it almost appeared that Themistocles wanted the group to provoke the Persians, forcing their hand. So here he was on what Themistocles termed the 'most important journey in the history of the Greek race' with an unclear understanding of what to achieve. After his performance on the island of Sicily, Eudox' confidence in his own abilities had rapidly declined. In order to recover his reputation in his own mind, Eudox had to be successful in Delphi. He believed his very soul rested on the outcome.

Eudox turned to Philokrates the Thespian, who was the named leader of the Greek delegation and had been traveling along side of him this day. The thespian was nodding off as the wagon continued on its bumpy path. Again, Eudox began to muse as his eyes focused on the man. Although he had a sense of the reasons underneath Themistocles' decision to bring an outsider on this excursion, Eudox assumed that Themistocles wanted the delegation to have the appearance of neutrality, and as representing the entire Greek culture. Themistocles knew that not only was the Persian anger based on the blood revenge of Marathon, but on the desire to burn Athens into dust. The die might have already been cast. Would a political solution douse the flame of Xerxes' anger? Deep in Eudox' heart, he didn't believe that anything would extinguish the hate that the King of Kings felt for the Athenian. But he guessed that it was worth a try.

Eudox' eyes left the thespian and focused on the sailor, Thantos, who was riding on a horse next to the cart in which they rode. An interesting man, he thought. He has unlimited bravery and an extraordinary ability to turn what seemed like a hopeless situation into a victory. He proved this on his journey as a spy to the heart of the Persian beast. Why was he the only man of four that survived the journey to Susa? And the information that he returned with outlined the strength of the entire Persian army and armada. A truly stunning feat. Eudox admired the sailor almost as much as he admired Themistocles himself. But he knew that Thantos was most comfortable on the water. And yet here he was taking a land journey to a diplomatic conference that would determine the future of all of Greece. The one thing he didn't understand about Thantos was why he was so devoted and loyal to Themistocles. Many times this sailor put his life on the line for this Greek politician. But, he thought, *I could ask myself the same question.*

Eudox knew that Thantos had no political aspirations or for that matter, he never spoke of even understanding the nature of the Demos. It was a mystery to Eudox. *"I have a political stake in this unfolding of history. But this Thantos, he was already a wealthy man beyond belief, so what was his purpose?"* As he stared at him, he concluded that there must be more to this sailor than was superficially obvious. Eudox admired Thantos' cunning and craftiness. He also instinctively knew that in a crisis, this sea captain could be counted on to stand and join the fray. Eudox' mind drifted again, finally settling on another area of confusion for him.

And then there was Lasiandra. Eudox asked himself, *"Who was this child and how did she captivate Themistocles' mind? Were the Gods really behind this person?"*

In such a short time period, this child gained the trust of a master politician who was able to outthink even the best strategists on the peninsula. Eudox did not really believe that this child actually communicated with the god, Demeter. But as he stared at this beautiful young child he thought, b*ut if she did, if she actually understood the contemplation of the Mysteries, she could be the most valuable member of this group.* Eudox mused, *Imagine if this child could actually give us a door to the knowledge of the Gods!* Eudox knew that the Goddess' insight could guide them through the delicate tributaries of political intrigue. How else could they defeat such an overwhelming military force that was most likely already on the track to their destruction?

There were times when this child, Lasiandra, appeared other worldly. She would descend into these protracted trances when it appeared her very soul disappeared from her body. She made strange whimpering sounds during these excursions. Sometimes these events lasted for minutes, and sometimes upwards of an hour. Eudox watched one of these long affairs with amazement. It bothered him for days, as he tried to understand what happened in this ritual. He was both terrified and mystified by watching this child. *This was the most confusing part of the journey; a mere child among these established men. Could she offer anything to the outcome? But if correct, her input could surpass the combined ability of all of these men. Remarkable!* He thought.

So here he rode, a puzzled man in an intricate and unclear situation. Themistocles had counseled him about the tasks that he would soon face. For sure, there were many layers to the enigma that now faced him. He would need all his wits and savvy. Eudox looked at the ground as it passed under the wheels of the vehicle in which he rode. He wondered, *would Delphi mark the beginning of the end of the Greek peoples? Or for that matter, would it mark the end of his days?*

He felt a chill. It was unsettling.

# Chapter II Aegean

The Phoenician, Sakarbaal, always woke early, as his sleep was restless, bordering on agitated. He had been put in charge of building, equipping, maintaining, and training the new Athenian navy. Progress under his firm and zealot hand was steady and prolific. He had already supervised the building of 100 triremes. The money was still available to build at least 100 more, possibly 150. Sakarbaal, who had been around ships his entire life, was taking great pride in the successes of both the builders and the sailors. Being a disciplined man, Sakarbaal spent many hours with the new Greek sailors, trying to instill within them the truth that unless the Greek ships had perfect coordination of their efforts, the numeric superiority of the Persians would crush the fledgling navy. The only hope the Athenian navy had was to be able to outmaneuver and out strategize the more ponderous Persian fleet. The men chosen to steer the Greek triremes needed to be the most intelligent of all the recruits. Sakarbaal also worked feverishly to develop a system of colored flags to communicate between ships. The captains gave test after test until they could master the intricate combinations. Sakarbaal wanted no mistakes. The Greeks needed precision in their coordination. But even with all of these preparations, Sakarbaal still had serious questions, not only about this fledgling navy's ability to defeat the Persian navy, but also whether they could even hold their own in a confrontation. At night he would wonder whether his thoughts were optimistic or delusional. On those nights, he would wake with a start and end up pacing until the morning light broke through his windows. Even with all his success, he remained a troubled man.

Sakarbaal stood at the docks and watched one of the newer ships being prepared for its maiden voyage. It was truly a beautiful structure and he treated all of them as a lover would delight in a newly found woman. To Sakarbaal, each of the ships held its own unique beauty. Although each of the triremes were built with the same template to the same proportions, Sakarbaal knew each of them individually. He had registered the slightest difference between the vessels. The men who studied under him were amazed at his ability to tell these one hundred identical sisters apart. Sakarbaal insisted that each of the ships needed to be named, for although he wanted coordination between the different vessels, he also wanted the sailors to identify with their vessel.

The Athenian trireme was long and sleek. There were three levels of oarsmen, all of whom needed to stroke in coordination. The captain stood at the front of the boat directing the course and tempo. In contrast, the Persian vessels were much wider and slower than the Greek ships. They relied on soldiers and archers which they carried for their firepower. With Themistocles' urging, Sakarbaal decided to follow a unique and distinctive design. The Greek ships did not have nearly the firepower of the Persian, but were hoping to be able to outmaneuver their enemy and render the larger ships useless by ramming their sides or cutting their oars off. This strategy was a calculated risk and had the possibility of miserable disaster. The Athenian ships were so light that on sharp quick turns, the sailors said they could feel the boat bend. But what the triremes did have was a heavy, bronze plated ram at the front of the craft. Every ship had at its frontage, a figure head of the Goddess Athena, each in a different position. Every man, either of high or low rank, had to bow to the image of the protective deity when entering the vessel.

Sakarbaal walked slowly across the docks. His mind was taken by distant thoughts of training and building. He strolled along the wooden planks, watching the water slowly splash along the sides of the docks. Seabirds flew overhead squawking uncontrollably. Sakarbaal was amazed at the unison of their motion, their sharp turns, and their ability to fly together, almost as one larger object. He was transfixed at this particular dance of these birds. This harmony was the template in his mind of how the navy needed to respond. He silently wondered whether this spectacular display had any purpose other than to make men jealous. He wanted his beloved triremes to function with such efficient harmony. He continued his slow walk, not noticing the figure approaching him from his rear. As a hand began reaching to touch his shoulder, Sakarbaal heard a familiar voice from behind, *"My friend, you look far away."*

Sakarbaal flinched when the hand touched him, but he quickly turned and recovered.

*"Themistocles, it is good to see you again, my friend."*

*"Friend? You finally see me as a friend?"*

Themistocles feigned surprise, but as he spoke, a long grin covered his face. Sakarbaal had to smile in return. The ex-Phoenician sailor responded, *"You are correct Greek, friend is too strong a word!"*

Themistocles laughed and patted the sailor on the back. As he did, he turned his gaze towards the beautiful ship that was passing in the channel in front of both men. He patted the Phoenician on the back as they both watched in silence.

*"You have much to be proud of. These ships are a remarkable accomplishment."* Sakarbaal became serious and peered into the politician's eyes. He then commented, *"These beauties might have a very short life. They have an almost impossible task."* Themistocles turned and said with a grin, *"Impossible maybe, but I prefer the word, unlikely."*

The two men turned away from the channel, and began walking toward the closest pub called, 'The Highest Light'. As they entered the establishment, they went to the proprietor and asked for a private room and a large jug of the finest wine. They sat for almost an hour and a half talking about varying subjects, ranging from the beautiful sunsets to the warmth of the lovely Greek women. Finally, the Phoenician looked directly at Themistocles and asked, *"Well, my friend, I know that you have something to say to me. You have never before made a special trip just to taste the wine with me. We have laughed and drank as brothers. It is time for you to tell me what the news is that you are not telling me."*

As he became more thoughtful, Themistocles responded, *"It scares me how easily you read my mind. But there is no bad news, just a question."*

*"I listen well,"* said the Phoenician.

*"Tell me, Sakarbaal, out of all the new captains, which two would you say are the most talented?"*

The Phoenician turned Greek collaborator thought for a moment and then said, *"The two most talented are Phile and Kallias. They are both smart and gaining more experience with every training run."*

*"But, tell me, Sakarbaal, are they ready for just a training mission or for real combat?"*

Immediately Sakarbaal responded. *"Yes, I have every confidence in their skill. But tell me what kind of mission you are considering."*

*"These words that I tell you, Sakarbaal, are not to be repeated, except to these two brave men. I have thought of this for many days. Our spies have informed us that the great Warrior Queen will be boarding a ship off the Persian coast heading for Delphi. I want our two bravest sailors to intercept her ship and sink it to the bottom of the Aegean."*

The Phoenician thought for a moment. In a pensive tone he asked, *"You have no faith that the negotiations will bear fruit?"*

*"No, Sakarbaal,"* Themistocles replied, *"I have all the faith I can in the talks that will be held by the great Oracle. But I also must be realistic. Sinking the Persian vessel will deny the Persian tyrant of his strongest ocean ally. I also hear that on board the vessel will be one of the great Persian military strategists. His name is Hamas. With one action we can remove two of their most experienced military minds. It is, Sakarbaal, a chance we need to*

*take. But I do want to be deceptive. I do not want this Artemisia knowing it is an Athenian vessel that attacks them. You can use any flag, from any of the cities that have chosen to deny their Greek origin and submit to the Persian subservience. I feel no guilt about undermining any of the alliances that have been so cowardly created."*

Sakarbaal turned away, clearly in thought. He finally asked, *"Whose flag should I use to disguise our ships?"*

*"I am sad to say, Sakarbaal, that you have many choices. The great Persian dictator has many submissive allies. I would suggest that you choose between those pigs from Thessaly. Eurphalus and his womanly brother, Thorax, were one of the first of the Attican areas to succumb to the Persian demands. The Aleuadae family are traitors at heart. Their blood is tainted. But you could also use the colors of the Egyptian or the Cypriots. They all follow the King of Kings like sheep."*

Sakarbaal again looked pensive. Finally he reacted, *"I will use the Egyptian. Their ships have been seen in the Aegean. It would not be surprising to run into one of their vessels."*

*"I will secure their designs for you to use. Summon your captains, Sakarbaal. They will need to leave immediately to insure that they will be able to intercept the Persian vessel."*

*"But wait, my friend. Before you make this decision to send these two men, I need to give you an extremely serious warning"*

With a clearly thoughtful look, Themistocles turned to the Phoenician.

*"Speak your true thoughts, my friend."*

Sakarbaal swallowed and faced the Greek politician

*"You realize that you are sending these men against the fiercest female warrior in the known world. She relishes pain and destruction. I know the oceans like I know my own skin, yet I would be no match for her on the open seas. She can sniff out deceit and will be merciless in her retribution. You might be sending these men to their immediate deaths."*

*"I am impressed with your empathy, my friend. In comparison to the Persian empire we are all ants under their feet. They can probably squash us without a second thought. Every encounter we have with them will be as the mole against the mighty snake. We will lose many souls. But in our position, my friend, we have nowhere to retreat to, no rock will be large enough for us to hide under. We must take many chances and hope that some reach success."* Themistocles took a step closer to the sailor.

*"If you are telling me that I am likely sending these men to die, you are probably correct, and it hurts me to think about that. But we must try and strike when even a small opportunity shows its face. We must be bold. Tell me, Sakarbaal, have you ever met a liar?"*

Now, with his face wrinkled in thought the sailor said. *"Of course I have"*.

*"I have known many liars. It's always been my impression that the more absurd the lie, the more it's believed. I have learned a lesson from this, that the bolder one is the more chance of success.*

*We can't stay timid in the face of such a threat. We must act with effrontery. Hesitation of action leads to failure, and in our case, slavery."*

Sakarbaal looked deep in thought at this lesson in power that was just offered him.

*"Remember, Sakarbaal, even ants can bite. Now, summon the captains."*

Bion cried for two days after Tryhon, the Pythia, her mentor and motherly figure left the earth, traveling into the great unknown. Bion was too young to assume the job at that time. She was the chosen successor to Tryhon, but she had to wait for a year until she reached 15. As the prophete, Bion had been taught daily by Tryhon. Her apprenticeship had lasted for almost a year and she was schooled in many aspects of the Pythia and her duties. As she was mourning for her master, Bion recalled and mused about many of the days and the lessons that the two women had experienced together.

One of the lessons that made a lasting impression on the young prophete was dealing with the Naiads. The Naiads were the female spirits that occupied the streams and rivers. The Pythia had to cleanse herself in the sacred river, called the Kassotis. The sacred Kassotis flowed under Apollo's temple and was thought to have mystical powers. This Naiad that lived in this holy water was one of the strongest, lustful enchantresses that occupied any of the sacred streams throughout Greece. The Naiad that inhabited the Kassotis was known as Tu.

Tryhon explained that whenever the Pythia entered the Kassotis to cleanse herself before her union with the God, it was Tu's task to undermine the rapture. Tu was a very powerful Naiad. She created a trance like state in the Pythia that, if given into, led to drowning and the loss of your soul. While in the river, Tryhon explained, one was infused with Tu's power and there was an almost uncontrollable urge to just give into the comfort of contentment. One could lean back and gradually accept fate, sinking under the water and becoming one with infinity. Tryhon worked hard with Bion in the mental practice she needed to resist Tu. During Bion's first attempt in the Kassotis, after a few minutes her eyes began to get a hazy look as Tu's enticing silently seduced her closer to extinction. As she faded, she started to sink under the swift current. At the last moment, Tryhon grabbed her by the shoulder, rescuing her from the clutches of the Naiad and sudden death.

In her mind Tryhon heard a low moan from Tu expressing her dissatisfaction that another soul was miraculously rescued. Tu had successfully taken a few Pythias in the past, and more than one prophete with her mesmerizing trancelike power. The seductive power of the water, along with the animus vapors, led to many a soul being lost forever.

Tryhon explained to Bion that there were many kinds of trances. The highest and most intense was the ecstatic rapture. But that level of connection with the God often left the Pythia close to death. The Pythia often went into seizure like convulsions during this high level rapture. Even Tryhon, with all her powers and experience, had only reached this level twice since being made Pythia. The safer rapture was a dreamlike state in which the Pythia left her body. Apollo replaced the Pythia and left the vague and obtuse message for the pilgrim. There were other raptures of course. The Dionysian Cult of the Dead was another form of intense rapture, as were the Elusion Mysteries. But out of them all, the blissful rapture with the God, Apollo, was by far the most powerful, and for that matter, the most dangerous. Tryhon went on to explain about the sweetness of death and the innate desire that we all have to return to the unknown from where we came. It was a compelling thought, and as we age, this desire strengthens within us.

*"We love the beauty of nature, and have a need to reach its perfection. There is a constant pull within us between life and death. It is not morbid, it is just fact."*

*"Do you know of death?,* Bion had asked

Tryhon rapped her arms around her apprentice and hugged her.

*"I know very much of death. Sometimes when I am in deep meditation, the desire to let go of life is quiet strong and compelling. Death always calls us, my child."*

*"Why do you resist its call?"*

*"I'm not really sure. The pull for life is just a little stronger. But I also know that the day will come when death will win the tug of war."*

The son of King Anaxandridas II of Sparta, and descendant from the great Heracles, always rode high in the saddle. The King, the 17th of the Agiad line, rarely left his glorious city except to fight. In all of Spartan history, this King was one of the very few to undergo the serious Agoge training required of all young men in their city. Only royalty was exempt from this arduous training. But the son of King Anaxandridas the II was not next in the line of descendants. His older brother was. So the young man went off to the Agoge. In his training, the offspring of King Anaxandridas II drew praise for his valor and uncompromising determination. He consistently scored at the top of the class in almost every training event, top of his class in almost every skill. He never faltered. He willed his way to the pinnacle of every competition he entered. He was the most accomplished swordsman and archer in the city. He practiced tirelessly, some days shooting 1000 arrows. In his early military forays of local disturbances with other cities, this young man led the charges and could out strategize even his own more experienced generals. His spectacular ability made many within the Spartan aristocracy jealous of his accomplishments. Rumor had it that Leonidas was actually descended not from Heracles, but from the great warrior, Achilles. When he heard of this rumor Leonidas said, *"Even the Gods can bleed!"*

Besides his physical attitudes, Leonidas understood power and how to control it. He made few close friends. He worried that if one became too close to others, it would be easier to be betrayed. No matter how harsh the situations appeared, Leonidas trusted only his own judgment. He also didn't want to become indebted to any person or faction. Other people didn't mold Leonidas, he molded them. This led to a cult like following, from both his friends and enemies alike. Nobody in the city outwardly criticized the King for fear of retribution. It became such that people would hesitate to challenge the great King, even in sporting events. Leonidas possessed a cold, piecing stare. It was rumored that he could burn a hole in people's minds with his gaze. But the most frightful thing about Leonidas was his bold approach to both political and physical conflict. Leonidas, because of his unrelenting self-confidence, would strike early and without hesitation. He secretly believed that the more audacious he was, the easier it was to overcome the enemy.

For over two hundred years, the Spartans were at odds with the city of Argos. Since the battle of Hysiase, the Spartans sought revenge for one of their few defeats. In a more recent confrontation, Leonidas had outflanked the Argos general and destroyed half of the Argivian army. At the time, Leonidas already was considered superior to other men, but this stunning victory only cemented his growing reputation and fed his hero worship.

As he rode with his entourage of 20 soldiers towards Delphi, Leonidas couldn't stop thinking about recent events that were evolving on the Peloponnese. Sparta had sent a representative to the meeting at Corinth where Themistocles was attempting to unify the Greek cities against the Persian menace. The Argives were one of the many Greek cities that refused to attend the meeting. The Spartans were so irritated by the cowardice of their traditional enemies, that when it was proposed that ambassadors would be sent to Argos, the Spartans insisted that a threat accompany it. They even went so far as to suggest that any city bowing to the Persian will, should be attacked and burned. It was agreed that any city that became Medized (agreeing to the Persian demands of water and dirt), would forfeit a tenth of their city's total income as a punishment for their treacherous ways. Of course, such a threat did not worry most of the cities as they reasoned that both Athens and Sparta would be overcome by the Persian horde, leaving no one to collect such a penalty. But the other issue that engrossed the Spartan King was a mystery.

A week before leaving Sparta a pair of blank tablets appeared at Leonidas' house. The envoy that brought them indicated that he wasn't sure where the message originated. But Leonidas recognized that on the side of the tablet was the sign of the ex-Spartan King, Demaratus. Demaratus, of course, was considered a black traitor by his birth city of Sparta. To many, he was just a coward who abandoned his city.

*"So,"*asked Leonidas. *"Somebody wants us to believe that a traitor is attempting to contact us."*

Gorgo, the King's wife, took the tablets and appeared puzzled.

*"My husband, these tablets are blank!"*

*"Yes, I know,"* said the King.

*"Somebody is playing a joke on us,"* Gorgo responded uneasily.

*"But even a joke has a purpose,"* said Leonidas. And as he spoke he turned to the back of the room. Deep in thought, Leonidas mumbled to himself.

*"A blank message. What is the significance of such an event? If it's from a friend, could it be a warning of some sort? If it is really from the coward, Demaratus, why would he want to contact me at this time? Could he know that I'm readying myself to go to the Oracle at Delphi to ask about our fate?"*

Not used to seeing her husband anxious, Gorgo spoke again. *"My husband, this is just a joke. You should not worry yourself about nonsense."*

Leonidas continued to pace, ignoring any inquiry. He eventually decided to bring the Spartan council in on the mystery.

The debate was frenzied. So what to make of this puzzling event? A day went by with arguments ranging from he was attempting to confuse and scare the Spartans, to the interpretation being that the blank tablets meant nothing could stop the great Xerxes. Some even suggested that the only purpose of the tablets were to prove that Demaratus was too stupid to write. Leonidas, in his usual manner, argued against the pervading feeling. *"My friends, we should not take our enemies lightly. Even though he is a despised politician, I hear that during the Persian invasion of Egypt he served with distinction. Our spies told us that he outfought the Persian generals. He is a dangerous man."*

Secretly, Leonidas felt some pride that a disgraced Spartan could outfight the Persian leaders. He wondered whether the King of Kings, was proud or angry at this happenstance.

*"Yes,"*

The King continued *"Maybe this disgraced man is shrewder than we think."*

He turned quickly towards the assembled senators and raised an arm to the sky.

*'Let us not underestimate a snake. Even when it looks asleep, it can still administer a lethal bite."*

And then, after hours of constant discussion, Leonidas' wife, Gorgo, in a moment of revelation, suggested that the wax that covered the tablets should be rubbed off. Leonidas looked in wonder at his wife's epiphany. He excitedly took the tablets to the table and began to shave off the wax.

As his knife slid across the tablet, a message miraculously began to appear under the wax. To the shock of those present, the message informed his former Spartan countrymen that Xerxes was, in fact, planning to invade Greece. It went on to outline the various military strengths of the Persian forces.

Many of the Spartan generals laughed at the numbers that were on the tablets.

*"It is impossible. Impossible to bring such a large force this distance."*

They refused to believe the enormity of the figures. They reasoned, therefore, that the only purpose of these messages had to be to frighten Sparta. Leonidas, not being a man who was easily intimidated, held a different view. He believed that the traitor, Demaratus, was actually trying to place his boat on both sides of the river.

Leonidas believed that the Persian King of Kings would bring Demaratus to Greece as any part of an invasion. He reasoned that the ex-Spartan could offer Xerxes strategic help, as he was familiar with the Spartan way of warfare. His reasoning continued that if the Persian overwhelmed the Greeks, then Demaratus would be in line to become the Persian governor of his home city. On the other hand, if the Greeks turned Persia away, then Demaratus could take some credit for the Persian defeat. Because of this, Leonidas trusted this message even less.

But as he rode to Delphi Leonidas thought, b*ut these numbers they are so exaggerated that no sensible man could believe them. But what if they are true?* Even for the heart of the great Spartan Warrior, such numbers were numbing.

Artemisia didn't expect that the feeling would be this penetrating. Although it wasn't obvious to others, the Warrior Queen shivered with anticipation. From the moment she smelled the ocean and then saw the blue-green water, she felt an undying urge to get back to the sea. She knew she missed the water, but her reaction was as strong as any physical experience she had ever had, easily eclipsing any organismic feeling that she recalled. She turned to Hamas, *"Do you smell it? Do you smell the aroma of the ocean?"*

The general gave an odd and confused look at this passionate woman

*"Do you know what that smell is? It comes from the plants that wash up on the shore. It is their mating smell."*

*"The mating smell of plants?"*

Hamas looked more and more confused and bewildered at this silliness.

*"All I can smell is the shit from the horses. I smell no plants mating"*

Although she knew she couldn't, Artemisia wanted to jump off this God forsaken horse and run to her boat. After the number of days of continual riding, the Queen couldn't feel her bottom. Of course she would never admit it, but the cramps in her legs almost brought her to tears. Then from a distance, she saw her ship, the Voltay, smelled the sweet sulfur of the green water, and she could swear that she heard the Voltay calling her. Miraculously, with the sight and smell of the water, the cramps disappeared and she felt energized. She knew she was home.

As excited Artemisia as was, the teacher Hamas, was equally emotional, but the feeling for him was anxiety. Hamas' hatred for the sea rivaled Artemisia's disdain for the horse. As the Warrior Queen stepped onto the Voltay her skin began to tingle in anticipation, as a lover waiting for the hard embrace of her man. Outwardly Artemisia almost smiled, although she resisted the urge. Her façade was more important to her than expressing her inner emotions. As she stepped onto the ship, she bent down and kissed the deck and felt its energy penetrate through her veins.

Two days out into the Aegean, Artemisia had once again gained her sea legs and was feeling back in control. As she stood on the deck at the beginning of the third day, Hamas stood ten feet behind, working hard to control his fear. Two of the Phoenician guards stood flanking the Warrior Queen. Without obvious prompting, Adon, the Phoenician overseer, turned to look at Artemisia. Hamas watched with the eye of a falcon, even though he was distracted by the distress in his stomach. Adon touched his head twice and then rubbed his right arm with his left hand. Still apparently looking out over the water, the Warrior

Queen reached her left arm to her lower back. Adon responded by touching his head again, then quickly rubbing his right ear and forehead. Artemisia made some unusual hand signals and turned her head and smiled at Hamas.

Later that day, Hamas rallied his courage and walked to the front of the ship. For a time he stood next to the Queen as she directed the ship. As he stood near, Artemisia began to speak. *"Yes Hamas, you are correct in your thoughts."*

The teacher looked surprised at the comment. Artemisia just smiled and continued, *"Come now. Don't try to hide your thoughts. I can read your questions before you ask."*

*"Yes,"* he said as she smiled.

*"And what am I thinking?"*

Artemisia looked at the teacher and said, *"Adon is worried about you. He says that you have turned green."*

Hamas laughed.

*"Did he mention how many times I lost my meals over the side?"*

Now it was Artemisia's time to laugh.

*"And what else did he say?"*

The Warrior Queen's mood became sobering. *"It is not something to worry about. Adon does not trust anybody who isn't comfortable on the water."*

Then, without warning, the Warrior Queen reached out and placed her hand across Hamas' chest.

*"What?"* said Hamas, in a shocked manner.

*"Shhh,"* she said covering his lips while the tension in her arm increased. In a lower voice she said, *"something is out there."*

*"I see nothing,"* said Hamas replied, wide eyed.

*"There is something there. We are being stalked".*

And she turned to her Phoenician brothers. In a flurry of movements, Artemisia communicated with them.

Some very tense hours passed in what seemed like minutes. It wasn't until late in the afternoon that Hamas was able to clearly identify the ship. Actually, there were two ships. They looked to be a few miles apart, and if Hamas didn't know better, it appeared as if they attempting to outflank the Voltay. But strangely, Artemisia did not appear concerned, and did not even seem to be avoiding the two approaching vessels. It confused the teacher, so he finally approached the Warrior Queen and queried, *"Tell me, Artemisia, do you know where the ships are from?"*

Smiling, the Warrior Queen hesitated and then said, *"their markings suggest they are Egyptian."*

She now turned her head to Hamas *"But they are not Egyptian."*

*"How do you know this?"* Hamas asked.

*"The Egyptians are experienced and good sailors."*

Pointing out into the ocean she said, *"These are not Egyptian sailors. These men are inexperienced. It makes me believe that they do not wish us well. They are attempting, to surround us in a very sloppy manner. They want us to believe they are Egyptian, hoping to get close enough to attack."*

*"But,"* said Hamas with an urgent tone. He expressed his concern, *"You do not seem to be aggressively trying to avoid them."*

*"Excellent observation, my soldier comrade. I do not avoid these children. I will play their game until I tire of it."*

She smiled at the strategic master. *"It is sometimes important to conceal your intentions in a combative situation. I am going to appear friendly and trusting. It is like baiting a pig."*

She laughed while looking at Hamas" *You see, my friend, I am not always impulsive. I sometimes believe that deception is the best strategy. Leading someone down a path is always entertaining for me. It makes the kill that much sweeter!"*

She then became reflective and sad *"I don't want them to see the fatal blow until it is struck"*

Kallias, the Greek captain, stood on the bow of his vessel and was fixated on the Phoenician ship that stood about five miles in front of him. He turned to his second in command and said, *"I think our disguise has worked. The Phoenician does not seem concerned about our approach. We will maintain some distance as the sun begins to settle. In the morning with the new light, we will take this Persian beauty. I have signaled Phile on the other ship and we will coordinate the attack. This will be much easier than I anticipated. At first light the Persians will be preparing to greet their allies. They are expecting a sheep and they will be greeted by a tiger. Tell the crew that it is time to rest. We have a long day tomorrow. Spread the word, any woman found on the Phoenician vessel should be killed. No prisoners taken. Place three guards on the deck. I need rest."*

Kallias smiled to himself as he went below.

It was an unusually dark evening as the moon was covered by low lying clouds. None of the sleeping Greeks heard the three people sneak aboard. The three guards were dozing when they lost their lives. The two large Phoenicians cut the throats of the sentinels and they died without knowing their assailants. The third man was purposely awoken by Artemisia. She enjoyed seeing the faces of those who would be losing their lives by her sword. She would remember their eyes and their sense of shock for days. She relished such an experience. She experienced more enjoyment from such an event than any sexual encounter.

The fallen Greek sentinel looked up at the Warrior Queen as she swung the sword, detaching his head from his body. She considered herself the perfect executioner. A smile covered her face as the man's torso fell gently to the deck. After standing for a few heartbeats to admire her work, the Warrior Queen silently walked over the deck of the Greek ship. She found shields, bows and arrows all of Greek origin. As silently as they penetrated the Greek defenses, the three Phoenicians left the vessel.

On the way back to the Voltay, the Queen smirked to herself again. The Greeks had fooled no one. She watched the dark sky while evaluating what she had seen.

*"I knew it,"* Artemisia said to herself.

*"I could tell by the way they sailed that they were not Egyptians. So the Greeks felt like they could get an advantage by sinking the Voltay, killing all its inhabitants. A smart strategy, I suppose, but naïve to think they could outwit me."*

She looked at the waves and swore, *"I know your hearts now. You don't have negotiations on your mind. Deception. These Greeks cannot be trusted. Their hearts are dishonest."*

She spit into the water. *"You will pay for this betrayal, my Athenian friends."*

She cursed at the moon with a sardonic smile.

Kallias awoke to find his deck covered with Greek blood from the three sentinels. Upon seeing the blood he somehow knew exactly what happened. He couldn't believe his stupidity, and he immediately lowered his head in disappointment. Sakarbaal had put his faith in him and he feared horrible failure. His commander came up to him with terror in his eyes and said, *"We've been attacked. I thought that our rouse was complete."*

Kallias looked at him with hatred in his eyes for pointing out the obvious. When he recovered his wits, his anger peaked and he screamed vengeance towards the Phoenician ship. But as he searched the seas, there was no Phoenician ship to attack. He cursed and looked a second time into the vastness of the water, hoping he had missed something. But with every breath, the truth of the situation became clearer in his mind. The Phoenicians were gone. They had sailed into the abyss of the ocean during the black night. Kallias wondered how this was possible, as there were not even stars to guide the ship. Kallias banged the side of his vessel over and over with unrelenting rage and disappointment. His commander approached him during the tantrum, and Kallias struck out at him, pounding his face until it looked distorted with blood. He had been outsmarted, outmaneuvered and shamed. All of this on his first voyage.

Kallias had hoped to prove himself and become a leader of the new navy. But now he would return as a humiliated and disgraced sailor. He had embarrassed his family and his lords. He assumed that he would be dismissed from the service and have to return to the damned sheep farm that he left for the sea. He looked down at his commander lying on the deck beneath him. The man tried to raise his head, but his eyes were so swollen he could barely see Kallias staring down at him with rage. Slowly, ever so carefully, Kallias removed his sword while staring down. He towered over his fallen comrade. Unhurriedly, Kallias raised the sword over his head. As he raised it up, he screamed to the Gods. The weapon came down as the commander lifted his arms to defend himself. To his shock and relief, Kallias impaled himself in the stomach. His screams rang through the vastness of the Aegean, as he twisted the weapon deeper into his body. His last words were, *'I cannot live with the shame!"*

Hieronymos woke with a start. Since he arrived in Delphi, his sleep had been restless. He dreamt vivid and strange thoughts. He saw himself flying one night, and during another, awoke terrified for fear of being eaten by a snake. He tried talking to the priest, Demonus, about his fears, but the old man only shrugged and said, *"It is time to grow up. Stop complaining about your childish dreams."*

In the two weeks that Hieronymos had been at Delphi and joined the Dionysian cult, he experienced things he never believed possible. From sunrise to sunset, the priests and priestesses all slept. But from the rising of the moon and the darkness of the evening, the dancing and consumption of wine was nonstop.

*"We are people of the night. You must get used to living in the blackness. The light only exposes weakness. You will learn the comfort of the darkness."*

Hieronymos could not have envisaged this type of reverie. Each night he drank to the point of nausea and had sexual experiences to the point of exhaustion. The diversity in the copulation was colossal. He was attempting positions and partners that even he had not imagined in his wildest fantasies. He was taught that Dionysus was nicknamed the Liberator, for he believed that these types of organismic experiences were the only way to free the true person from the overly socialized self. Whereas the fools of the Elysian Mysteries believed that deliverance came from internal contemplation, Dionysus knew that emancipation came from losing the self in a trance like sexual experience. The only true exploration of the soul did not involve turning inward in meditative thought. It did not arise from long ocean journeys of spiritual thoughts, but from releasing the bodily spirit in sensual explosion. Although his dreams were wild, and at times frightening, Hieronymos slept deeper than he had ever had when he was home.

To reach states of perfection, Hieronymos drank potions that he was told were made from herbs and mushrooms. During one of these experiences Hieronymos found himself copulating with two other men. The intensity of this experience was greater than any he had achieved with women. From that point on his preference was solidified, even though he inherently knew it before his journey to Delphi. As he experimented with this type of practice he found that pederasty was his favorite. He felt most at home copulating with older men. They used shafts called olisbas which made Hieronymos tremble with a mixture of pain, pleasure and contentment. Since then, he continually sought out such arrangements, especially with the older priests who also favored this delight. He seemed to be their favorite.

Hieronymos recalled in his hallucinatory dreams that he hatred his father. Analyzing this in his mind, he rejected the idea that this was in any way connected to his growing enjoyment of the olisbas. After a while, Hieronymos boldly rejected any advances by woman as that began to disgust him. His reputation for his preference grew with every passing night. He seemed to relish the blood that was often associated with the experience. The boundaries between pain and pleasure became blurred, merging together. Without really noticing it consciously, the pleasure associated with sensual experiences became associated with the experience of pain. When Hieronymos thought about this, he believed his feeling of rejection from his father probably led to this habit. Violence was now linked with love.

Even though his first contact with the cult was Demonus, the aggressive and offensive priest, Hieronymos developed a strange attraction to this narcissistic man. It seemed that the more abusive the priest was to him, the more Hieronymos secretly desired him. He would fantasize about his first encounter. Finally one night, Hieronymos built up his nerve and approached the older man. As Hieronymos entered Demonus' room, the old priest almost ignored his arrival. Then Demonus commented, speaking as if he were talking to the wall.

*"Why do you waste my time with your presence?"*

Shocked by the greeting Hieronymos stood silent, immediately wondering whether he'd made a terrible blunder. And yet this feeling of rejection was somehow familiar to Hieronymos. Finally, after a few minutes of silence, the priest turned his head toward the young man. *"Your ears are plugged with shit?"*

Hieronymos seemed to compress into his own body. His head bowed and his shoulders seemed to sag inward. The priest smiling to himself, slowly walked toward the young man. He grabbed Hieronymos by the hair and forced him down to his knees. Almost shaking, Hieronymos grabbed the priest's calves and tried to hang on. Demonus bent over and whispered in the young man's ear.

*Do you like the pain?*

Almost imperceptivity, Hieronymos nodded his head. The old priest began sweating, but he tightened his grip and almost lifted the young man off the floor. He then put his arms around Hieronymos' chest almost pressing all the air out of his lungs.

Now, face to face, the priest asked, *"Tell me, is your ass tight and ready for me?"*

*"Please!"*

Hieronymos begged. The priest began slowly licking his face and took the young man to his bed. With every step, Hieronymos felt the strength of this priest entering his body. His hands were so strong and powerful that Hieronymos felt himself harden under the touch.

# Chapter III- Delphi

Philokrates, the Thespian appointed the leader of the Athenian delegation, and Eudox were becoming very friendly on their ride to the great Oracle. At one point, as the group was finishing supper at one of their stops, Philokrates asked, *"Tell me, Eudox, what do you know about this Oracle that we are visiting?"*

The Athenian politician looked in surprise at the Thespian.

*"Do you mean to tell me that you know not of the reputation of the Pythia?"*

*"What is the Pythia?"*

Philokrates looked confused at his response. Eudox looked vacantly at him and thought, *"This is the man that Themistocles decided should lead our envoy? "*

But as he stared, his mind quickly had an epiphany.

*"No, no, Themistocles is much too smart. He must have had an underlying reason to choose such a naïve emissary. Themistocles is much too forward thinking. I wonder if he has already concluded that these negotiations are meant to fail?"*

Eudox's mind was shocked back into the present by Philokrates asking, *"Eudox, Eudox, are you here or dreaming?"*

Eudox's face immediately changed to recognition.

*"I am sorry, Philokrates. I was dreaming. My mind is questioning the importance of what we are doing."*

*"Eudox, please, I am bored with this journey. Tell me all you know about Delphi."*

*"All I know, Philokrates? If I did that you would truly be bored."*

Both men laughed. Philokrates began, *"I assume Eudox, that we are going to a temple."*

*"What?"* Eudox said, again surprised by the stupidity and elementary nature of the question.

*"Actually Philokrates, there are two temples in the same building. The one for the God, Apollo, faces east and the rising sun. The other, for the God Dionysus, faces west and worships the night."*

*"I never heard of two Gods existing in the same temple,"* Philokrates commented.

*"They are brothers,"* Eudox continued. *"But they represent the different sides of the same circle. Apollo represents thought and reason, whereas Dionysus represents pleasure and sexual drive."*

Eudox paused for a moment and then decided to give the Thespian some information. *"It is said that millennia ago, father Zeus released two heavenly eagles to search out the center of the earth. They flew for days eventually settling on the side of Mount Parnassus. It was deemed the center of the world. It is here that Apollo fought the great serpent and claimed the area for his Oracle. In Apollo's temple there exists a conical stone marking the exact center, called the omphalos. It is placed in the specific spot that the blood of the serpent spilled over the ground under Apollo's sword. I have heard that on both sides of the omphalos stand two solid gold eagles sent down by Zeus himself. It is the holiest place on earth. It is from here that the God communicates with man. The Delphic Oracle has been reading the future for almost 1500 years. Remarkable, isn't it?"*

Philokrates was overcome. He listened intently and was obviously impressed by the sheer life of the Oracle.

*"Tell me, Eudox. The Oracle's predictions, are they usually accurate? I have heard that Apollo preaches to us through the Oracle."*

Eudox again smiled at his friend.

*'Over one hundred years ago, one of the great sages of Sparta, Chilon, approached the Oracle. Chilon was in quest of knowledge about the nature of man himself. He asked Apollo what was the best for mankind. He further asked, how can a man reach nirvana? '*

Apollo answered through the Pythia with just two words, ***"Know thyself"***.

Again awed, Philokrates pressed his lips together in thought. Eudox continued, *"During another pilgrimage to the Oracle, Apollo was asked how a man should know what to do if confronted by two decisions. The Pythia, revealing the God's thoughts said, "He should wish to learn from experience, and then the truth shall be revealed to him".*

Philokrates, looking less serious commented. *"Well, my friend, it would seem that asking Apollo a question is a dangerous mission."*

*"Dangerous?"*

Eudox inquired.

*"Yes, dangerous, my friend. The truth is always dangerous. It is much easier to be deluded than to confront what the future*

*holds. Would it be better to live a deluded, happy life, than a fearful and miserable truthful one?"*

"And I thought this man was naïve", Eudox mused to himself. Finally, Eudox said, *"Over the long life of the Oracle, Apollo gave four consistent messages: Know thyself; moderation in everything; learn from experience; and, all misery is in the mind.*
*"*

The two politicians stared at each other and smiled. Finally, Eudox became even more serious. *"I have been told, my friend, not to underestimate the power of the great Oracle. It has, in the past, been able to dispose Kings with its revelations. It is said that empires can rise and fall, but the Oracle is the one constant in our changing world."*

Eudox continued, *"I do find it ironic that the God has chosen a woman to relay his thoughts. I have often pondered this inconsistency. We Greeks tend to disregard the thoughts of women. Another thing that bothers me is that there are many Oracles attributed to many of the Gods. But the others all depend on hidden signs. Zeus is purported to make his wishes known through the rustling of leaves. A strange way for a God to act."*

Eudox touched his head and heart at the irreverent comment. But he continued. *"I have also wondered why Apollo has been chosen to present the clearest messages."*

There was no way for Eudox to know that, as he spoke, green eyes were watching him from the heavens. Athena was laughing silently at the questions that the Greek was bringing up. She turned to Bubo, and the owl flapped its wings.

*"Do you hear this, my beauty? Do you hear what this man is thinking? Men are such fools!"*

Bubo squawked and flapped his wings in agitation.

*"Yes, my love, my father Zeus, as well. These men do not realize that it is their female God, Athena, who has conquered all, risen above all of her male counterparts. They are blind my love, and will probably remain so for some time. I cannot change their course."*

As the clouds began darkening the sky, again Bubo appeared agitated. *"Don't worry my love, my father can read my thoughts. But I can also read his. I love scratching his skin and irritating his nature. It is part of my remaining joy."*

The Goddess stopped and her eyes turned luminous as she stared at the man who was musing on his trip to Delphi.

*"No, my love, I will not intervene. We are facing turbulent times my love. It is exhilarating. My interference will only calm the waters. No, no, Bubo, I will not force Apollo's hand. He is in his glory now as history emerges on him. Although I have a sense of the future, I will enjoy how he handles these conflicting questions. No Bubo, my hands must be kept clean"*

The Goddess smiled. *"At least for the time being"*

The son of King Anaxandridas II, the 17th of the Agiad line, and the descendent of Heracles, was the first of the delegations to arrive at Delphi. Although he would never admit it, he was tired of the voyage. His journey had been slowed because of the wagons of gold and silver that the Spartan brought to pay homage to Apollo and his Oracle. He believed, as all Spartans did, that the weight of the gift would bring a more favorable response from the Oracle.

As he approached Mount Parnassus, the Spartan delegation purposely stopped there rather than entering the city proper. Leonidas had an ulterior motivation other than to rest the animals. As the sun set in the western sky, the king left the encampment with two of his warriors, announcing that he needed to practice his sword play.

Sword practice was a religious ritual in Sparta, and Leonidas took it very seriously. Perfecting balance and skill in this popular practice was a lifelong dedication for a Spartan soldier. For Leonidas to be leaving the encampment during dusk would not be an unusual event. Leonidas worked very hard on the different hand pressures of the various killing strokes. The Spartan teaching regimen dealt with the transfer of energy between the legs and the arms. Leonidas' sword was special with a magnificent pearl handle. Not a straight blade, the sword had a slight elbow bend half way down its shaft. Its handle was gold plated and Leonidas doted over it, keeping it as sharp as possible. Leonidas' balance was extraordinary, which made him the perfect killing weapon with the sword.

The three Spartans walked almost a quarter of a mile outside of the camp. This was a patterned practice, not one of those in which the King took on two or more people, with only one of the four men leaving alive. Often captives of wars were used in the practice session with the incentive being freedom if they could kill, or disarm the king, none of whom ever won their freedom in this exercise. On this early evening, the practice lasted almost an hour. Leonidas stood in the center with the other two flanking him. As they approached, the king fell to a knee and parried both of their initial advances. He rose with his right arm bent and the sword resting on his shoulder. The battle continued, with Leonidas twice stopping his blade within inches of each of the men's throats. At these times he would smile, standing frozen for a second, so the man understood that in real combat his life would be over. All three men were drenched in sweat from the forceful workout. As they lowered their swords to finish the routines, the king said, *"Return to the camp. I will stay here and meditate for a while."*

The two slaves bowed to their sovereign, but looked surprisingly at the king, as it was unusual to leave the ruler alone when not in Sparta. Leonidas gestured with his arms motioning them to leave. The men bowed again and touched their heads, indicating their recognition of their king's orders. The two slaves both slowly left the practice field, not once looking back at their king. They both knew that, even though it was a direct command from the King, if something happened to Leonidas, they would pay with their lives.

Leonidas watched the men leave and then slowly walked to the small patch of woods east of their position. He sat under a tree brandishing his sword and waiting. Two hours went by and the King heard sounds coming from the forest. It sounded like human footsteps, not animals. Leonidas stood and placed his sword in the ready and slowly moved behind the tree he was leaning against. Two men suddenly appeared from amidst the bushes, and quietly the King had identified the position of the sound, allowing him to sneak behind them. Like a cobra beginning to strike, Leonidas emerged from behind a tree catching the two men off guard. Before either of the men realized what was happening, his sword was firmly placed under the neck of the taller of the two men, while the other man stared in shock. Then a broad smile came across his face and he shoved the man forward. Both men immediately dropped to their knees and placed their heads on the ground.

*"Rise,"* the King demanded. Both men stood, while the man who came under Leonidas' sword was still trembling.

*"Tell me what I need to hear,"*

Leonidas asked intently.

One of the men looked up and said, *"My King, two delegations approach the great Oracle."*

Leonidas' eyes widened imperceptibly.

*"Keep speaking"*

*"Lord, one of the delegations comes from Athens and the other from Persia."*

*"Persia?"* The King immediately stopped, looking stunned by this information.

*"Persia, my lord. We are assured of it."*

Leonidas turned quickly facing the two men. His eyes were aglow with an emotion that seemed like expectation.

*"Tell me more of these Persians."*

*"My lord, the delegation contains a woman that is rumored to be a great warrior. They say she is undefeatable."*

Leonidas' expression turned to anger as he quickly moved forward on the man. Again his sword ended under the man's throat.

*"Remember with whom you speak. You are standing in front of the greatest warrior of his time. And you have the gall to say a woman is stronger than I? Surely the Gods have rotted your brain."*

The man quickly dropped again to his knees.

*"I am sorry, lord. I do not mean any affront to your power. I just relate what is told to us."*

Leonidas grabbed the man's hair and pulled his head back. With fire he said, *"Keep talking, but watch your words carefully."*

*"Lord, along with the woman, It is rumored that the Persians have sent one of their top military planners. Also, the Persians have released many spies we assume to gauge the strength of Greek resistance."*

The King, smiling to himself, realized that the Persians were coming no matter what their motivation was to go to Delphi. Leonidas knew that he had a big role in fueling the Persian vengeance. When the Persians sent an ambassador to Sparta demanding earth and water, the usual Persian custom of asking for subservience and servility, the Spartans threw the envoy into a pit and let him starve to death. The Spartan King knew that such an affront could not go unpunished. It rivaled the animosity that the Persian King, Xerxes, must feel about the battle of Marathon for the Athenians. A traditional rival, Leonidas couldn't let Athens outshine him in any area. But no matter what the King of Sparta felt about the Athenians, he silently admired them, for like those of his city, they were standing up to the threat without fear or timidity. He knew that the majority of the Greek cities bowed to the Persians before any army stepped onto their soil. Leonidas was disgusted by these cities. Rather than fighting for their pride, they groveled in the face of the threatening Persians. He spit on the ground thinking of these traitors.

Leonidas relished the thought of facing the great Persian army. He had told his confidants that he believed Xerxes needed to be humbled.

*"He is a self-righteous child."* The King of Sparta mumbled, as he walked away.

Returning from his muse, Leonidas turned back to the two spies who stood in front of him. With a snarl he said, *"This woman, it is rumored that the Goddess Athena, has taken human form. Is this the woman we speak about?"*

*"We know not, lord. We have heard that the woman is a Phoenician and is very aggressive in her battles."*

*"We will see,"*

thought the son of King Anaxandridas II and the 17th of the Agiad line

*"We will see."*

He spit on the ground three times and his cough shook his body. His lungs were now usually congested. This condition arose after his arduous and extended stay in the dank prison of Susa. On some days his breath was so short, he had trouble leaving his now shabby residence. He coughed so hard that he needed to hold onto the nearest stationary object or else he would fall to the ground. Sometimes he witnessed his own blood coming from his lungs as he hacked into the night. His body was dying and he knew it. He could feel it in his bones. He knew the time was nearing. But there was more to do.

Ningizzida hoped that his body could last until he was able to revenge himself against the petulant Persian King. Walking around Babylon almost brought tears to the priest's eyes. The city had been so beautiful. The gardens, the structures, the great tower, were all now leveled. Even the walls of the beautiful city were now gone. The city was now dying like the old priest himself. In the Persian vengeance for the botched revolt against their rule, Xerxes sent one of his armies to punish the Babylonian peoples. They assumed incorrectly, that such a thrashing would humble the Babylonian people, bring them into line and discourage future uprisings. But they were wrong. What it did was not to humiliate, but strengthen the Babylonian will. Before the aborted revolt, the Babylonian peoples had proudly been part of the vast Empire. But now, the Babylonians saw the Persians as invaders and foreigners. Men would spit on the ground after a Persian passed. In private they referred to them as, 'outlanders'.

Ningizzida's popularity blossomed to a God-like status since the Persian genocide. Over half of the Babylonian population was killed or enslaved by the Persian. One might think that the

Babylonians would have placed some of the blame on the old priest for the Persian revenge. But just the opposite happened. The stories about the priest who took on the great Persian despot were widespread and growing daily. He was seen as a ghost, a messenger from God, who the King of Kings could not destroy, or even find. He and his followers had killed many Persians in the preceding months, but the numbers of the men from the east were endless.

Ningizzida had mixed feelings about prayers. The stories about his abilities had reached such heights that people were now offering prayers to him, rather than to the God. It was said that he had the ability to bring the dead back to life and heal the sick. There were stories of his escape from the Persian dungeon, when the priest was covered in light, rose miraculously up to the heaven. It was also rumored that Ningizzida could transform people, turn them into ghosts and spirits. Of course, Ningizzida did little to dispel any of the stories or myths about his abilities. He relished in them, actually beginning to believe that many of the tales actually occurred.

Ningizzida had achieved the status of the God's legate on earth. Although these beliefs were encouraged, Ningizzida felt some deep shame and guilt. Luckily, these feelings were not entrenched enough within his soul to create anything other than a fleeting moment of remorse. Many nights, other lesser priests, acolytes, and town elders would gather to hear the recounting of many of the mystic's stories and tales. Ningizzida was especially focused on his ability to travel the night winds and enter the souls of others.

One of his favorite stories was of a man named Oxathres. Oxathres was a civil servant in an eastern town named Bactra, on the Oxus River. Ningizzida recalled in his story telling, how the soul of Oxathres wife, Parmida, reached out to him in a visionary event. He was meditating one evening when a vision appeared. The woman, whom he described as having long straight hair, but only half a face, emerged out of a rock. She was bloodied, and green pus flowed from her remaining eye. She approached the stunned Ningizzida, falling to her knees in front of the legendary priest. Her voice was, '*as if stones filled her mouth*'.

*"You are the great one."*

Ningizzida sat in silence staring through this strange aberration.

*"I have come to you to beg for my eternal soul. I was married to my husband Oxathres, for many years. I believed him a good man, always providing bread for myself and his children. But one day his spirit became infested. Tiamat took over his being. He began drinking and coming home beating myself and his children. As I protested this behavior, his wrath grew more and more assaultive. Many nights I cried in my own blood, holding my beaten children. Oxathres burned my face off one night when I challenged his whereabouts. My corporeal being passed into infinity three full moons ago, at Oxathres' hand. Great one, I come before you pleading. Since my passing, two of my young children have joined me in the clouds, also from Oxathres' vengeance. I plead with you, Sheshgallu, for justice, for myself and my children"*

Ningizzida would rise at this point in his story. He would raise his arms to heaven and speak in the forbidden language of the ancients. His voice would rise and his tone would vibrate off of the walls. His arms flailed, his voice gaining an eerie tone, as he dramatically recalled his story.

*"I could not let such an injustice stand in the face of God. My soul twisted and seized at the thought of Oxathres' behavior."*

The Sheshgallu crouched in his retelling, spread his arms and lowered his voice in a theatrical fashion. His eyes seemed to float in their sockets as he made eye contact with everyone listening to his tale. He went on," *That very night, I entered Oxathres' mind as he slept. I created an illusion that he thought was the truth. There was a large mountain near Oxathres' home. I created the thought that God wanted Oxathres to climb the mountain. God foretold that when he reached the summit he would hear the word of the Lord."*

Ningizzida now lifted his body and pointed to the listeners. *"The next day Oxathres climbed the mountain as he was instructed. When he reached the pinnacle, Oxathres stood and looked into the deep valley. His legs shook with his fear of the height. But a voice came into his mind assuring him not to be alarmed. His legs trembled as he was urged to move closer to the abyss. Oxathres was now sweating, worried that he would lose his footing. The voice continued in his mind urging him to step forward, over the edge. Oxathres looked up in protest, fearing that if he took a step forward he would plunge downward, dying in the fall. The voice was persistent, assuring Oxathres that God would not let harm come to him. Oxathres closed his eyes and stepped over the edge."*

The Sheshgallu ended his story, rising and walking away from the others.

*"Wait,"* they called *"Wait Sheshgallu tell us what happened to Oxathres."*

Ningizzida stopped and turned to the people who had gathered to listen to the tale, and with a fiery expression said, *"What do you think happened?"*

The people watched in silence and the Sheshgallu continued, *"He found salvation in his punishment."*

On this morning, the ancient priest waited by his bedside for one of his underlings to bring him breakfast and report any rumors that were circulating around the city. Ningizzida already knew that the Persians had sent an entourage to Greece to consult the great oracle at Delphi. The group had stopped in Babylon on their way to the Aegean. Although Ningizzida did not really comprehend how the King of Kings could benefit from consulting the Greek Oracle. He was now convinced that Xerxes had made up his mind not only to vanquish the Greeks, but to destroy them. In watching how he handled both Egypt and Babylonia, there was no doubt in the old priest's mind about the intentions of the King of Kings. He meant to burn Athens to the ground, as he had broken and liquidated his beloved Babylonia.

Ningizzida knew that the invasion of Greece caused great risks for Xerxes. Bringing the war to the distant Peloponnese would take a Herculean effort, not only to transport the immense army, but to defeat the Greek resistance once there. Such a military effort could bankrupt the empire. In any case, Ningizzida believed that the only reason for this invasion was to satisfy Xerxes and his father, Darius', revenge. But no matter what the result, the attempt would seriously weaken the strength of the empire. Ningizzida knew that the defeat at Marathon by an inferior Greek army burned in the hearts of the Persians. The Athenians rubbed salt in the wound by erecting a building to honor this great victory. Ningizzida understood bitterness and retribution. The priest reasoned that Xerxes' burning desire was to destroy Athens to regain his own honor.

*"Such a fool,"* the priest thought. *"This spoiled boy-King would destroy everything that was built over three generations, just for glory."* It made the old priest pleased to know that Xerxes would dishonor his heritage just to prove a point.

But Ningizzida also knew that within a weakened Empire, other cities and provinces would begin to pull away and challenge the strength of the Meads. At full strength and in peace, holding such a vast empire together was a formidable and unenviable task. A weakened Persian Empire, with its armies spread across the known world, almost guaranteed insurgence. Ningizzida relished the thought. But he also planned to take advantage of the time Xerxes was chasing his elusive revenge in Greece. While the King of Kings was on this sojourn to satisfy his blood lust in the Peloponnese, Ningizzida planned to set up an underground network of support, eventually striking out again at this King of Kings. He purposely failed a chance to poison the young King before. He would not be so foolish again. Next time he wouldn't waste the opportunity.

The old priest sat in the back of the cottage in which he lived. His mind was wandering as he sat still in his daydream. He was grateful that his God had granted him the strength to live this long. He prayed to God that he would be allowed to walk the earth for at least as long as it would take to revenge himself against the young King.

Ningizzida meditated for some of hours. Finally he fell to his knees. From underneath his robe he revealed the sacred candles. The candles came from the Ziggurat temple at Ur. They were the same candles that Ningizzida had always used to read the divine smoke. Two hours before, the priest had drunk the special mixture that was needed to free the mind and communicate with the God. As he sat on his knees he unsheathed a knife and slowly, ever so slowly, he began cutting lines on his arms. The blood would serve as a personal sacrifice to his God, Marduk. As the liquid of life began oozing from his skin, Ningizzida felt his mind drifting into the world of the spirits.

Ningizzida looked up to the heavens, raised his arms, and pleaded, *"My lord, I am here, your faithful servant, the keeper of your ceremonies, the Erib-biti. You have allowed me to become a Kalu, granting me the power to change fate. I have defeated Tiamat, the one who lives in the darkness of men's souls. Fear and desire have no control over me."*

*"My lord, I understand the pure Apsu, the place between your realm of heaven and the world of the land. The Assyrians, the Mesopotamians, the Babylonians, and soon the Persians, bow to me and your strength, lord. And I lord, your dedicated servant, bow to you. I have achieved the highest rank that a priest can attain, that of Sheshgallu. I have learned the secrets of the sea-land peoples, and I comprehend the seven creation tablets of the Enuma Elish, your greatest gift to man."*

*"My lord, you have allowed me to escape the shackles of the ungodly infidel Persians. With your help I have escaped death. And now I sit here, lord. Allow me to enter your thoughts. Teach me about the path that you want me to travel. I know that the path is unclear, and I have struggled at times. Show me the way, lord.*

*Allow me to route the meads and expel them from our land. From your heavenly city of Babylonia, the Persians have destroyed the godly image of you, melting it down and turning it into profit in their hellish city of Susa. In our victory I will rebuild your heavenly city. The walls will be greater and whiter than before, the gardens will bloom more spectacular than ever, the tower will reach to the clouds."*

*"It is time, lord. The final battle is approaching, and your servant, Ningizzida, is ready to carry your flag. Lead me, lord. Take the blood of my body, my savior. It is my gift to you. I offer my life to prove that I am yours. Give me the wisdom of your thoughts."*

He lowered his head.

*"I will have my revenge!"*

And the old priest then allowed his blood to drip into the sand, making himself one with the land.

Hieronymos began the seven mile walk to the caves. It was a difficult journey, for it was mostly uphill on small rocky, paths. He still hadn't recovered from the revelry of the previous week. His head pounded as he slowly trudged up the steep walk, repeatedly stopping to reclaim his breath. Hieronymos had become close with some of the other young men in the sanctuary. In total there were 12 initiates, and this night would mark their ascension to full membership in the cult. Although not having an easy climb, Hieronymos was quite excited. His hair was braided with long red ribbons reaching down almost to the ground. All of the initiates had colored ribbons, but Hieronymos' were the only bright red ones. He was proud of his distinction, as he was told that he was chosen to have a special part in the upcoming ceremony.

The Dionysian ceremony was highly laden with many solemn and primordial procedures. Strict attention was paid to tradition as old liturgical songs from archaic languages were sung and acted out. The obsolete languages and traditions that were used had their origins in the Dorionic tradition. There were Hittite influences as well, and a written language was used that bore resemblance to the Phoenician script.

As they reached the mouth of the cave, the women and priests were already involved in celebration. It appeared almost to be daylight inside the cave, as there were torches and candles that reached deep into the bowels of the earth. The smell of smoke permeated everything. Hieronymos noted that the women and priests were dressed in their finest garbs. The priests wore pearly white robes with black stripes down the back. Their heads were freshly shaven, some with blood dripping down the sides of their faces. The women outnumbered the men by at least two to one. They all wore short dresses that barely covered their private parts. As the initiates entered the cave, the women formed a line so they could walk between them. They swayed seductively, offering their breasts to suckle as the initiates walked by. As the young men passed, some of the women turned away and bent over exposing their behinds, pulling their cheeks apart, begging for the men to enter.

Hieronymus and the other young men were led to the back of the cave where a makeshift room had been set up. Demonus entered the room with a large clay pot filled with a mixture that all the initiates drank from: This mixture was different than the typical mixture that was consumed at other ceremonies. Its effect was almost immediate, as Hieronymus began hallucinating, losing touch between himself and others.

Demonus, the head priest of the order, walked among the young men, massaging their genitals as he passed. He then led the initiates out of the tented area. As they left, Demonus put his hand on Hieronymus' chest indicating to him that he was to stay behind. Hieronymus made eye contact with the old priest, and after waiting for the other men to leave, Demonus slowly walked to Hieronymus. He came eye to eye with the young man, and said, *"You are a beautiful young man."*

The priest reached down and cupped Hieronymus' testicles. He smiled. *"They feel warm in my hands."*

He grabbed Hieronymus' hand and gently pulled it down toward his groin.

*"Do you like these?"* Demonus asked. Hieronymus sheepishly nodded. With his other hand he patted the young man on the cheek.

*"Are you ready for your ascension?"*

Hieronymus again nodded in approval, but his mind was flowing through the vastness of space. The priest gently squeezed to the point of some pain. The young man raised up on his toes as the priest lifted up with his hand.

*"Well, my pretty, you will be honored tonight. You will touch the God tonight."*

As the young man stared into the eyes of the older man, the priest took two flasks from out of his robe. He handed them both to Hieronymus. The priest said, *"You wait ten minutes after I leave you. You drink the blue water first. After you have swallowed the entire flask, drink the red flask."*

The priest quickly turned and left the room. Hieronymus followed the instructions of Demonus and he felt his limbs and lower body numbing.

Hieronymus was dizzy as he was led out of the room. He saw colors and the walls of the cave seemed to move as he walked. Everyone in the cave seemed to walk with him waving their hands over their heads as they danced their way to the center of the cave. Some of the men were holding Hieronymus up as they walked, as his legs felt separated from his body. As they neared the center of the cave, Hieronymus noticed a table was stationed in the center of the room surrounded by candles of all shapes and sizes. He wasn't sure how many candles there were, as the lights seemed to merge and dance into a continuous stream. It felt like there were a thousand hands moving up and down his body, and Hieronymus was unable to separate one from the other. It almost felt like his body was covered by slithering snakes.

Hieronymus was led to the table as the ensemble mass yelled and screamed dancing around him. He had never felt so special in his young life. Most of his life was spent avoiding people and people avoiding him. When he had made the decision to join the cult, everyone called him fool. But now, look what has happened. Everyone was focused on him. He was not alienated, he was revered. His mind swirled, not staying on any particular subject. Many of the men gathered around Hieronymus and lifted him off the ground. With Hieronymus in the air, his hair waving around him, the men danced around the room. The woman fell to their knees when Hieronymus passed. The wine flowed and Hieronymus was given gulp after gulp as he was paraded up and down the sides of the cave. As the men lifted and brought him down for more wine, Hieronymus felt nauseous, almost throwing up during one of the passes by the statue of Dionysus.

On the next pass, the men brought Hieronymus to the table. He was almost thankful as the table felt secure and would hopefully allow his head to stop spinning. At least he wasn't moving anymore. He almost didn't notice that his arms and legs were being bound by felt ropes, as he really couldn't feel his extremities. His mind continued to drift, as wine was slowly poured into his mouth. All the woman took a pass, walking around Hieronymus, kissing him seductively, opening and closing their mouths on his lips. Their tongues darted in and out of his mouth, and to Hieronymus' surprise, he began to stiffen by the wet touches. Demonus slowly pulled Hieronymus' robe open and began to slowly stroke his stiffened penis. The priest tightened a small leather belt around the base of his penis, keeping it rigid. The priest was gently stroking the shaft, slowly milking it. Then unbeknownst to Hieronymus, Demonus slowly pulled a shiny knife from under his frock. The women continued to moistly kiss his neck and mouth, shielding Demonus from Hieronymus' sight. The priest then began to slowly lick Hieronymus' penis, forcing it to become engorged.

Out of everyone's sight, Demonus raised the blade. The knife quickly cut the engorged member off the semi-conscious young man. Being engorged, the penis squirted blood everywhere. Demonus held the member up to the sky and the assembled throng screamed with delight. Hieronymus jumped from the sharp searing pain, but his arms and legs were tightly bound, and he was unable to move. His screams were muffled by the chanting and singing of the revelers around him. Demonus continued to hold the now shriveled penis in the air and chanted:

*"Our devotion to you is boundless Dionysus.*

*We offer this sacrifice to prove our sanctimonious affection.*

*Give us your power with this pious sacrifice*

*Bless us Dionysus "*

The crowd shouted

*"Bless us Dionysus*

*Bless your loyal disciples."*

The pain between his legs was so stunning that Hieronymus quickly lost consciousness. His bloody penis was passed from person to person, as they screamed in ecstasy in touching the dismembered body part. The woman covered their lips with the blood.

Demonus, now covered with blood, stayed between the unconscious young man's legs and cupped his testicles. His eyes remained focused on the hairy scrotum. He then reached down and slowly, almost lovingly, cut the testicles off Hieronymus as well. Again he raised them to the sky and chanted to the God, Dionysus. Although Hieronymus was still unconscious, Demonus walked up toward his face. He bent over him and quietly, so nobody else could hear, whispered: *"Well, my beauty, now my penis is the only one that you will ever have."*

The seventeenth of the Agiad line and the son of King Anaxandridas II of Sparta, rode into Delphi at the head of the large Spartan column. He wore his most impressive armor and sat as straight as he could on his white stallion. The horse, raised by Leonidas, appeared to understand his position and the status of the man who sat on his back. The mare pranced along the stone walkway that eventually led to the Temple of Apollo. This was unusual for the Temple of Apollo lay at the top of the mountain. The path was winding and difficult to navigate. During the ride, Leonidas passed many different structures, each built by a separate Greek city to hold gold and other sacrifices for the great Oracle. There were also over 100 statues of Gods, Goddesses and heroes. As Leonidas entered the sacred pathway, he suddenly halted his approach, ordering his entourage to return to the city. There were protests from his guards, but the King raised his arm and all objections ended. The temple was not noticeable from the city, sitting almost a mile and half above the city and back in a cove. Leonidas was now completely alone without any protective cover. He slowly led his horse to the base of the great temple. The animal appeared anxious, apparently understanding the importance of the King's arrival. Leonidas dismounted and slowly climbed the steps to the temple, passing the statues of the Gods that guarded the entrance. Leonidas bowed his head almost imperceptivity as he pass each golden statue. He almost looked as if he was daring the Gods to turn him away, as his face snarled in front of a few of the statues. Eventually the Spartan King approached the columns that surrounded the entrance. His walk was slow and calculating. When he was within ten feet of the entrance, the King fell to one knee and removed his helmet. He placed his sword on the ground in front of him in an offering to the God. He kneeled silently with his head bowed in admiration. After a while he rose and bowed again in deference to Apollo. The King then deferentially withdrew from the temple, backing away from the steps of the entrance. It was very unusual for a Spartan King to take backward steps. They did not do it in war, and did not do it in politics.

That evening, Leonidas relaxed on his first evening in Delphi. Three virgins were brought to the King and he satisfied all. The Spartan delegation's accommodations were quite luxurious. The Spartans were always very generous in their 'donations' to the great Oracle. Because of the popularity of the Oracle and the accuracy of the prophecies, Delphi was most likely the richest city in all of Greece. It was almost shameful how opulent the city was. Even on this occasion, Leonidas brought wagon loads of gold and silver to satisfy the God. This reputation of generosity translated into epicurean delight for any Spartan that entered the city. To have the great King of Sparta travel to Delphi was unusual, in and of itself. The rumor that Leonidas was heading to the Oracle created quite a stir in the local establishments. Most people were aware of, and threatened by, the possibility of the Persians sweeping through the Peloponnese. And then suddenly, probably the greatest warrior on the Peloponnese arrived at the great Oracle to ask about the future. The Spartans were also granted special considerations about speaking to Apollo. Whereas, others had to wait days and sometimes weeks to ask their questions, the Spartans immediately moved to the head of the line. Therefore, on this first evening, Leonidas was preparing to speak with the Pythia the next morning. He had no doubt that he would not have to wait long for such a meeting.

As he relaxed after his affirmations to the God, the King was wiped down from the sweat that covered his muscular body. He donned a white robe to rest for the evening. His respite was interrupted by a slave who requested to enter his room. The slave, bowing furiously as he entered, reported that a priest from the Oracle was in the waiting room wanting to speak with the Spartan King. When the priest entered, he graciously bowed to Leonidas, reporting that his name was Akakios. The priest said, *"Lord, I am honored to be in your presence. The God, Apollo, welcomes you to his glorious city."*

Leonidas, with a self-righteous look, didn't move an inch at the priest's statement. Akakios continued. *"Lord, in two days, the Pythia will hear your question."*

Leonidas jumped up from his couch, and in an aggressive manner quickly moved towards Akakios. The priest instinctively backed up in face of the King's advance. Leonidas looked as though his eyes would burn through the now frightened cleric. In a very aggressive and angry manner Leonidas said, *"The King of Sparta is not used to waiting two days. I am wondering who is in this city that is more important than the son of King Anaxandridas II of Sparta. My people have worshipped Apollo as long as existence can remember. Tell the Pythia that the 17th of the Agiad line will arrive at the temple tomorrow at the point of the sunrise."*

Summoning his courage, Akakios looked into the face of the angry Spartan and said in a stuttering voice, *"It is impossible, lord. The agenda for the next two days is already set. Lots were drawn for position. I cannot change the results."*

The King took two mighty steps until his mouth almost touched the nose of the priest.

*"The King will arrive at sunrise. I will not wait longer. Remember priest, the Spartan sword is more comfortable when it is covered in blood. Much of the gold that sits in your coffers came from the Spartan body."*

Akakios swallowed deeply and backed out of the chamber.

True to his word, Leonidas arrived at the Temple as the sun broke over the horizon. He was met there by two priests, and without fanfare or confrontation they led him to the holy waters of the Kassotis to be purified. He was accompanied by the priests as well as three slave girls. As Leonidas slowly removed his amour and underclothes, the three slave girls quietly gasped at seeing his naked body. They seemed to take forever, as they slowly purified the King in the precious water that ran under the temple. As this ritual was being performed, the priest chanted the sacred rhymes. Leonidas was forced to leave his armor and weapons and wear the ceremonial robe that all pilgrims to the temple had to wear when seeking a reading. The King felt naked without his weapons, but he understood the custom and bowed to the request.

Leonidas was led into the temple proper. As he entered, a message appeared carved into the stone. It read:

**If you enter here, know thyself.**

A small table appeared in front of him. It was covered with colored flasks of warm wine laced with tonics. The King eagerly drank from the bottles in the specified order explained by the priests. The floor was made from polished stone that was refined to the texture of glass. They were cold under the feet of the King. As he was led down the hallway to the inner sanctum he noticed the beautifully sculptured columns that surrounded the gallery. In the center of the rectangular passageway lay the temple hearth. By this time, Leonidas noticed that he wasn't steady on his feet and he realized that the wine contained more than just the juice of grapes.

The hallway was dark as the ceiling was low, only a few feet above the King's head. A tubular vent was built into the ceiling above the hearth, allowing the smoke to spiral out of the temple. The fire in the hearth was lit and crackling. As the King approached, the warmth of the flames seemed to overwhelm him, reaching deeply into his bones. Leonidas was having difficulty concentrating as he found his mind being overcome by celestial visions. He saw humanoid figures floating through charcoal colored clouds. Lightening seemed to flash above his head, illuminating paths of smoke along the ceiling. The hallway smelled of burning wood as he strode forward, putting great effort into remaining upright. No matter what he ingested, the Spartan King would not allow himself to falter. The Spartan never retreated and never gave into weakness.

At one point Leonidas saw a large bearded face appear in his mind and his legs appeared to detach from his body. The visionary face overcame his consciousness, and the voice encompassed his mind without the lips moving. The eyes of the vision were liquid and had no pupils, but they stared through the King. In his mind he kept hearing his name repeated over and over in a low undulating voice. The voice seemed to be urging him forward, but all he heard was his name.

Eventually, Leonidas approached the sacred laurel that lay in the center of the wall in front of him. Reaching the laurel, the priests fell to their knees to pray and offered sacrifice to Apollo. The room was now quite dark, as the son of King Anaxandridas II of Sparta fell to his knees in prayer. His head spun and he wanted to lay to his left. A mist seemed to emerge from the stone wall and low choral chanting filled the air. The chanting was in a low repetitive baritone in which Leonidas joined in. Flashes of light appeared, and as he lifted his head, Leonidas noticed an opening to the right of the laurel. He stared at this space as the walls had appeared solid only a second before. Leonidas kept blinking in a vain attempt to clear his vision.

After a few minutes the priests helped the Spartan King to his feet and led him to the opening that miraculously seemed to appear out of the mist. Leonidas hesitated before entering, as the opening appeared to fall away without solid ground underneath. The priests had withdrawn leaving the King alone. The voice in his mind demanded that he step forward. There were only a very few times in his life that the son of King Anaxandridas II of Sparta felt a twinge of fear. Walking into a void, confused, without weapons, qualified as one of these unique and unusual moments. He had never recognized the feeling before, but now he identified it. But this ephemeral moment was transient, as the King stepped gingerly forward into the emptiness. To his surprise, his feet touched a step in front of him. Slowly, and with as much focus as Leonidas could muster, he walked down what his feet identified as stairs. He silently counted 15 until the floor straightened out. Finally a dim light appeared from a side of the room he was in, and Leonidas reached down and felt a bench. He instinctively sat, wavering, but holding his body upright with his strong, tree like arms. Leonidas' head still felt light and he had a strong urge to sleep. But the King resisted and remained steady. Finally two priestesses appeared and gently took his hand. They led him out of the room and his eyes focused on a gold statue of Apollo in the opposite corner of the adyton or inner sanctum. Next to the statue of the God was a flat stone marking the grave of Dionysus, Apollo's amorous brother.

On the left of the golden statue stood a small four columned edifice under which sat the Omphalos. The omphalos, that mythical monument that marked the center of the earth seemed to glow. When the King's eyes focused on the sculpture, the story of the origin of the clay piece came into his mind. As a child Leonidas was taught the story of how Apollo defeated the large python that guarded this holy place. Delphi had been rumored to be the center of the earth. It was told that it held such importance that Zeus sent a large serpent to guard its powers. Apollo defeated the serpent and it retreated to the underworld. Apollo then took over the holy ground and named the priestess the Pythia, to honor his strength and his victory over the serpent. The Omphalos was large, the size of a man. It was rumored to be hollow. It was thin at the top and it widened at its base. Its artistic design was a series of ropes tied in knots. On the side of the Omphalos sat two golden eagle sculptures which represented the duel raptors that Zeus released to find the center of the earth. The Omphalos was located on the holiest place in the entire Greek world.

Although Leonidas' head was beginning to clear, the situation still felt surreal to him. In the corner of the squared room was the famous tripod, positioned directly opposite of the Omphalos. It was as yet empty, as no priestess sat on the large chair. The King knew that the Pythia was the only one to occupy the tripod. Leonidas was told that it was tradition for the pilgrim to be on his knees when the voice of the God appeared. The Pythia was only a messenger in the flesh, not worthy of any attention. But at the voice of the God, her power rose to the heights of omnipotence. But even though omnipresent, the God, Apollo, spoke only through the Pythia. Other Gods communicated with humans in different fashions. Athena sent familiars, or at times, she herself took on forms to influence the course of human events. Zeus spoke through the winds, and Demeter had her mysteries. Apollo read the future through direct and obtuse messages. It was up to the humans to interpret and take actions from the messages.

The seventeenth of the Agiad line and the son of King Anaxandridas II of Sparta sat in front of the tripod. His eyes alternated between hazy sight and drowsy half dreams. In between his altering states, a deep green fog appeared to engulf the entire area. Leonidas really did not know whether he was viewing an apparition or a real person. But as the fog began to clear, a woman appeared, seated on the tripod. Leonidas raised his head and was shocked by the vision of the female. Even though his thinking was clouded, Leonidas couldn't help but notice the beauty of the woman seated in front of him. Instinctively he stared at her, although she appeared to notice his presence, nor his gaze. Her face was clear but her form was diffuse. Eventually the woman spoke.

*"My name is Bion. I am the Pythia. You have come in front of the God with questions, Spartan. What do you want to know?"*

Leonidas raised he head. A glow appeared around the Pythia's body. It seemed to originate from each of the walls, meeting simultaneously at the Pythia. Bion spoke again, *"Ask your question human, Apollo has arrived."*

Leonidas felt a chill. He swallowed and spoke, *"What is the future of Sparta?"*

The Pythia threw her head back and began a shrill chanting. She alternated between laughing and howling. The trance seemed to last for hours, but only minutes passed. Then in a deep, almost masculine voice, she said, *"Your Fate, O inhabitants of the broad fields of Sparta*

*Is to see your great and famous city destroyed by the sons of Perseus*

*Either that, or everyone within the border of Lacedaemon*

*Must mourn the death of a King sprung from the lines of Heracles."*

It took an hour or so for Leonidas to fully regain his senses. He appeared to drift between lucid thoughts and irrational mumblings. He was led by the priestess to a room in which he could recover from the ordeal. He was exhausted from the experience and gave in to the need to sleep. When he awoke, the seventeenth of the Agiad line and the son of King Anaxandridas II of Sparta were concerned about what the Oracle had said. A priest had entered and read the response to the King, as many pilgrims were unsure about the message, which was at times drowned out by the hallucinatory experience. While the priest repeated it, Leonidas had remembered it, almost word for word. But hearing it from the priest, made the message more ominous because of the emphasis that he put on several words.

Leonidas knew that the God was speaking to him directly, warning him that his life was in danger. This did not instill fear within the King's heart. Death was a celebration for the Spartan, especially if it happened during the protection of his beloved city and kingdom. It was almost exhilarating for the King to ponder. The son of King Anaxandridas II of Sparta knew that war was approaching. He believed that the Persians were in Delphi just for show. They were feigning the desire for compromise. Leonidas understood the passion of conquest. It was a difficult drug to avoid. Once a King tasted victory, he would create conflict just to experience the exhilaration of subjugation. The young King of the Persian Empire was coming. Leonidas knew it. He could feel it in his very essence. He was warned by Demaratus of the strength of the Persian sword, but there was no force, not of man or divine origin, that worried the King of Sparta.

Leonidas recently dreamt that he stood in a field when he saw the Goddess Athena, standing opposite him. The Goddess spoke, *"You have come before me, King of Lacedaemon, on the banks of the Eurotas River. My enemy, Ares, the son of Zeus and my brother, has challenged me for superiority in Olympia. This is not a worthy combat for me, for I have embarrassed my brother many times. I have chosen you, son of Anaxandridas, to be my hero."*

*"But Goddess, your brother Ares is the god of war itself. How can a mortal face an Olympian."*

*"Are you scared, Spartan?"*

*"Scared, Goddess?"*

*"Scared, Spartan!"*

*"Would you have sent for me if you saw fear in my heart?"*

And as these words left the Spartan's mouth, a figure appeared in the distance, the God, Ares, wearing his full extent of red armor. The bellicose God began laughing as he saw the King of Lacedaemon standing opposed to him. The God carried a large spear that glowed with a red mist. The God, known for his irrational rage, approached the King, towering over the monarch. Ares looked at Athena and said, *"You expect this puny human to oppose me!?"* Ares continued to laugh as he pointed toward the King. As the God of war looked toward his sister, Athena, Leonidas unleased his sword, piecing the God's armor. The King's dream ended with the God Ares, staring at the Spartan spear protruding from his chest.

It was this dream that reinforced Leonidas' vision that the Goddess, Athena, held him in her heart. Such security only strengthened the King's inner harmony, convincing him of his ability to resist the Persians.

When he returned to his residence, a slave told Leonidas that two people had dispatches for him and were waiting to see him.

The first man was a member of his entourage and told him that the Athenians and Persians had arrived at Delphi and were also expected to speak with the Oracle. The second man was more intriguing. Leonidas had never met this man, but he wasn't a slave or a eunuch. It was quickly evident that the man was educated, as he held himself differently than a man in a lesser position. In proper reverence the man entered the room and quickly bowed his head to the Spartan King. He waited for Leonidas to give him permission to speak. Leonidas was curious at this man's purpose. Finally, he raised his arm indicating that the man could explain his presence.

*"Lord, my name is Diodotos. I am honored to be in your presence. The Spartan race is to be admired for their strength and discipline."*

Stoically, the King looked at the emissary. The man continued, *"I am sent here by my master to beg a summit with the great Spartan King. He suggests it would benefit both peoples."*

Smugly, the Spartan King said: *"I need no benefit."*

The King turned his face away from Diodotos.

*"Lord, I beg you to give my master a meeting."*

Leonidas turned back to the man and asked, *"And who is your master?"*

*"Lord, I am sorry, but my instructions were to keep secret the name of my master. He is concerned that others in this city wish him harm. I am supposed to leave this message for the meeting place with you. I beg you though, lord. Consider this meeting. If you decide to meet with my master, it must be surreptitious. He urges that you take steps to make sure nobody else is aware of this meeting or follows you to its destination."*

Fire rose in the King's eyes. *"Are you suggesting that I meet with an unknown man, come unguarded, and make sure nobody is aware of my presence?"*

*"Put in those terms, it does not sound like a prudent thing to do,"* Diodotos responded. Leonidas paused and paced around the room. Finally, he spoke again.

*"Tell me, Diodotos, are you from Attica?"*

*"No, lord, I am not"*

*"Where are you from, Diodotos?'*

*"I come from the city of Chalcis, on the island of Euboia"*

*"Chalcis?"*

*"Yes, Lord"*

*"Are you from a prominent family?"*

*"I am, lord. My grandfather fought in the Lelantine wars."*

*"Are your family traders"*

*"We are, lord."*

*"Then you have sailed the Euripus Strait?"*

*"We have, lord, many times"*

*"I hear, Diodotos, that the waters of this strait are calm to transverse."*

*"It is not true, lord. It is a very treacherous passage. The tides turn quickly. The waters could pull you in one direction, and then without warning, shift into another. It is quite dangerous"*

As the man backed away, the King was intrigued by this obtuse message. His questioning led him to believe that Diodotos was a truthful man. The Euripus Strait had the reputation as a destroyer of ships. As Diodotos left, Leonidas said, *"Tell your master I will be there. But also tell him that I will be armed."*

The Persians had arrived in Delphi the night before. The Warrior Queen was still seething with anger at the events that occurred on the Aegean. She had been difficult to be around, and there had been many confrontations among the travelers. She wanted blood. Twice she had to be pulled off accompanying slaves as she threatened lives at the least provocation. The way from the Aegean to Delphi had been longer than anticipated. When the mountains surrounding the city were seen, the Queen seemed to begin to calm, although in her heart she wanted to return to the sea. Besides the brief confrontation with the supposedly Egyptian boats, the entourage had a confrontation with pirates off the island of Kythnos. As was usual, Artemisia spotted the pirate vessel before the others. It had been hiding in a minor island cove off of Kythnos. But once it was apparent that the pirate vessel was stalking them, the Warrior Queen chose not to run. As was her pattern, she decided to play dead. When the others protested against this strategy, Artemisia responded, *"If I run I project weakness. I want my strategy to be unexpected and concealed. Preparation against a dead ship leaves the hunter confused and bewildered. He becomes overconfident in his superiority. He becomes clumsy."*

The pirate ship rushed the Voltay as it drifted in the Aegean Sea. They rushed in only to be bitten by the deadliest snake on the open sea. Between the Warrior Queen, Hamas, and the Phoenician Warriors, the Voltay easily overcame the pirate vessel. Prisoners were not taken. The most attractive of the pirates was sacrificed to the Gods. At the end of the battle, Artemisia caught the warrior, Hamas, smiling at his joy of the bloodlust. She winked at him and began to laugh when his face distorted at the gesture.

Since their arrival, most of the entourage rested and celebrated the end of their long journey. The exception to this was the eunuch, Ummanaldash. During the journey the eunuch had been quiet, staying in the shadows. He avoided much of the contact with either the Warrior Queen or the teacher, Hamas. He tried making himself invisible. Therefore, when the group arrived in Delphi he was able to slip out of their rooms without being missed. His intention was to try to mix in without causing a stir. He was armed with plenty of gold and silver to grease the tongues of the locals. His mission was to find as much information that he could about the Greeks. He also was to meet with some of the many Persian spies who had been planted in both the Peloponnese and in Attica. In reality, many of these operatives were not Persian, but came from many of the Greek cities who had already given the water and sand to the Persian. This symbolic ritual sealed many of the Greek cities to ally them with the empire. Ummanaldash had been studying the language of most of these cities for many months. He believed that the Persians were coming in force to conquer this area, and his job was to lay the foundation and establish underground connections.

Ummanaldash wandered the city searching for specific individuals. On the second day of his cloaked meetings, Ummanaldash met a man named Lysim in an ally in the poorer section of the city. Lysim was a grizzly man, dirty and unkempt. He was missing his left eye and wore a leather patch over it. In their first brief meeting, Lysim spoke for a time telling the gruesome story of losing his eye. The way Lysim told it, the loss happened during a knife fight over a woman. Lysim had come from a small city south of Athens. He had no loyalties, except maybe to gold. Lysim had been working for the Persians for two years, being enticed by silver and gold coins. He had saved much wealth, which he hid away in a hole in the wall of his house.

Lysim met Ummanaldash for the second time in a field outside of Delphi. Ummanaldash had promised to bring a large jar of wine as part of their arrangement. Lysim guzzled the wine, and he smiled at seeing the eunuch. After a while Lysim said, *"Tell me, Ummanaldash. I heard you are a eunuch. Is this true?"*

Blushing, Ummanaldash nodded his head. Lysim smiled and looked down at Ummanaldash' crotch.

*"Let me see!"* he said.

*"What?"* protested Ummanaldash.

*"Pull up your robe. I want to see. I don't believe it."*

Ummanaldash stared at him, not knowing what to do. The Greek walked closer to him and said, *"I have a surprise for you, but I will not show you until you lift your robe."*

After a short while, the eunuch looked at the sky and slowly pulled up his robe, revealing his crotch. The Greek bent over and studied the area as if he was viewing a prized bull. He then laughed, rose, and roughly patted the Persian on the back.

*"Good! I had to make sure that you were who you said you were."*

He said, *"Come, Ummanaldash, it is time to go."*

The eunuch looked surprised and said, *"Where are we going?"*

*"We ride, eunuch. We ride to Athens."*

# Chapter IV- Epistle

The sun shone through the trees creating a halo of light on the ground. There was some movement of small birds, but the water that flowed through the garden was quiet on this day. She stood with her legs shoulder length apart and bent. Her arms were out in front of her body with her left hand facing her heart and her right hand facing away from her body. Her arms were bent and the back of her hands touched each other. Her eyes were closed as she focused inward. Although her thoughts were centered on the garden of meditation, in this visualization Lasiandra envisioned a small temple that she had visited. The temple housed the Goddess, Demeter. Lasiandra would imagine conversations with the Gin which she sought guidance regarding certain issues. The Goddess would tell her that the solution to all problems lay in her heart, and the search needed stillness and silence to be understood.

This day was different. Lasiandra had sunk very deep within her meditation. She felt herself slipping away into a dark void. She felt her heart slowing and she began to lose consciousness. But as it occurred, she did not feel her ephemeral body collapsing. She felt nothing of her physical being. All of her awareness was now resting in her mind. She had lost touch with everything else. She didn't even know if she was still standing. She opened her eyes within her mind and she saw clouds. Beautiful reddish and pink clouds.

A voice became conscious in her mind.

*"Are you happy, my child?"*

*"Happy?"*

*"You have made great strides, my young one, but be careful. Your life is about to change."*

Lasiandra had been standing for ten minutes when an internal sense forced her to begin opening her eyes, breaking her trance. To her right, and only a few yards away, sat a woman with her legs crossed. As Lasiandra opened her eyes, she saw an older woman staring at her. The woman spoke. *"I have seen you in my dreams. Tell me your name."*

*"My name is Lasiandra."*

*"Lasiandra,"* the woman said in contemplation.

*"Lasiandra,"* she repeated.

*"Yes, yes,"* she continued, *"I have seen you before. Apollo has told me about you. I was anticipating meeting you."*

Lasiandra was surprised by the comment.

*"Apollo?"* she asked.

*"Yes, my dear. I am Bion, the central Pythia."*

Understanding immediately, Lasiandra walked over to the sitting woman and bowed in adoration.

*"Sit next to me, Lasiandra. I wish to know you in the flesh. You are the young woman who understands the Mysteries of the Demeter. "*

Lasiandra nodded.

*"I saw you in your trance. I was able to see you in your meditation. Do you always go to the castle?"*

Lasiandra again was shocked by Bion's comment.

*"How did you see that?"*

*"Remember my dear that I have direct contact with Apollo. For brief periods I see what the God sees, know what the old knows, feels what the God feels. You have learned from the Goddess, but Apollo enters me. It is a merging you cannot imagine. Much greater than your trances and your visions."*

Lasiandra continued to stare at the older woman. Bion smiled and then continued. *"I will tell you one of the secrets of eternity. There are many layers of the Gods. With the Mysteries, you can reach the second level. At this level you can reach into yourself. The Gods will transverse all of the levels of existence. When the Gods take over your body and mind, you have the opportunity to experience all seven of the layers."*

*"What is it like?"* Lasiandra inquired.

*"I really have difficulty explaining it with words. But let me say this, because of the intensity, your life leaves your body during the experience. You can wander around any of the layers, speak with all the dead, and learn the secrets of existence. Space and time merge together. There is experience and attainment. You go from a human searching for becoming, to achieving a God-like state of being."*

In a stuttering response Lasiandra asked, *"Can I experience the God?"*

*"I'm sorry, my dear. It is a complicated process. But the hardest part is defeating the Naiad's"*

*'What are the Naiad's?"*

Bion smiled again and placed her hand on the young girl's shoulder.

*The Naiads are nymphs. They are the daughters of Poseidon and have many powers. The Naiads are very seductive, but the one that inhabits Kassotis, the holy river, is one of the most vengeful. Her name is Tu. In order to reach rapture with the God, Tu must be vanquished."*

*"Let me tell you a story, Lasiandra. Many ions ago, there were three virgin sisters called the Thriae. Melanina was called 'the black'. The second sister was Kleodora, who they called 'the gift'. The third was Daphnis- called, 'the Laurel'. Kleodora mated with Poseidon. Melanina mated with the God, Apollo. Their child was*

named *Delphos, which gave the name to Apollo's oracle. You see, most believe Delphi was named after the snakes. But I tell you a secret, it was named after the God's child, Delphos."*

Lasiandra was absorbed, listening to the history from Bion. Suddenly the Pythia interrupted her thoughts and said, *"But I know what you are thinking. Don't even consider it, Lasiandra. Tu is a formidable adversary. In order to have any chance to defeat the nymph and gain the ability to have rapture with Apollo, you must learn and practice for years. Look at me, Lasiandra. You must not attempt what you are thinking, as you will not defeat the nymph."*

Lasiandra looked blankly into Bion's eyes. She had already made up her mind to make the attempt. Again Bion forced her to look into her eyes. With a sterner voice she said, *"If you are convinced to try, I will not be able to help you. You will be at the nymph's mercy."*

*"I am going to try."*

*"I know you will,"* Bion said.

*"Will you at least let me go with you?"*

*"You can, Bion. I will go this evening."*

*"Are you sure I can't talk you out of this? For if you proceed, it could be your last day on this earth."*

The young Greek woman nodded her head and a tear appeared in Bion's eye. She knew in her heart that the end result was already predetermined. She had to figure a way to interfere with the outcome.

*"But you must promise me, Lasiandra, that when we go you will follow my instructions. If we do things in a certain order, your chances of success will improve."*

That evening the two young women were both dressed in ceremonial robes. It had taken two hours for slave girls to put their hair in curls on top of their heads. They walked hand in hand on the winding trail below the temple to the holy water of the Kassotis. The crystalline water moved swiftly over the rocks of its bed. Bion had stood in this place many times, as the Pythia cleaned herself in this place before the rapture with the God. They both stood watching the flow of the water when Bion said, *"Before entering the water, we will both meditate. I need you to return to the castle."*

After getting her directions, Lasiandra settled into her meditative stance. She had become well practiced at her contemplation, and before long she was walking to the visionary castle. The sun felt hot on her warm skin as she realized she was naked. This was an unusual change, as she had never been without clothes during her meditative experience. After noticing the modification, the young girl continued to walk slowly to her usual position. She was surprised when she arrived and sat in the lotus position that another presence was in front of her. Although there was no form, Lasiandra could feel the essence of the being. She was not scared of the premonition. But as she tried to understand what was happening, a low voice very quietly appeared in her mind. Although no sound existed, the voice said, *"I can feel your strength, Lasiandra. Tonight your life changes forever. Stay to the warmth, child, stay to the warmth."*

Lasiandra felt as if her insides were ringing. Shock waves passed through her, as if they were temperate winds blowing through her chest. The feeling was euphoric, and Lasiandra began drifting over the castle. But as she sank deeper and deeper into her own mind, a different experience emerged. Something was touching her back. The force seemed to pull her downward and she struggled not to leave her trance. But the force was too great and she opened her eyes to find herself grounded in her stance next to the sitting Bion.

After a minute or so, Lasiandra put her hands down and faced Bion. They both stared at the stream and the colored mist that appeared over its surface. It seemed to shimmer and slowly change colors. Lasiandra stared at the mist and then switched her attention to Bion. Bion looked at her and pointing at the mist said, *"The Nymph has arrived. Don't be confused about the beauty of the colors. The Nymph is a changing rainbow. She hypnotizes you with her beauty. If you give into her visual charms, she will sap your energy."*

Lasiandra bowed her head in understanding. Then, without hesitation, she boldly took her first steps toward the river. For the moment, the water felt comforting. Lasiandra moved without indecision, deeper into the flow. The mist seemed to follow her, almost stalking the young woman as a crocodile would slowly follow a gazelle. Lasiandra turned to the mist and opened her arms, inviting it into her body. The mist touched her skin and she felt a slow, icy sensation moving up her arm. She immediately found that her eyes became itchy and unfocused. Her head almost flew back as the mist began infusing itself within her body, entering every pore of her skin. Lasiandra's skin began to emit a bluish tint. Inside her mind, Lasiandra heard laughing growing louder with each few seconds. Her arms and legs became numb and she began floating. She could feel the energy draining from her body as the water began to spread over her face. Her resolve seemed to evaporate. Without knowing it, Lasiandra had already accepted death. In fact, there was calmness about her body as she slowly began to sink. The laughing grew, and without realizing it, Lasiandra was no longer in control of her thoughts. Before releasing all of her volition, she remembered the voice from her meditation say, *"Stay to the warmth, child."*

Lasiandra could almost visualize the vitality flowing out of her limbs. With her last bit of strength she attempted to recover the fleeing life energy, stopping its impetus towards the blue mist. She wrapped the remaining volition in her body around the fleeing warmth. But it was of little effect, as the laughing and draining grew more encompassing. The little strength and resolve she had left quickly began evaporating. The blue mist was now permeating her very existence. As the last bit of red energy started down her arm to leave her body forever, an outside force intervened.

In the response to the intrusion, the mist immediately coagulated into a vague human form. The expression was enraged. The nymph raised her arms, and in a violent display of fury, doubled her size. Behind the floating Lasiandra stood the Pythia with her arms now crossed, staring down the mist. In a graveled voice the apparition bellowed, *"She is mine, you have no play here!"*

Bion grabbed the sinking body of her new friend, lifting her back into the oxygen.

*"She gave herself to me by her own volition. You cannot interfere,"*

The Naiad, Tu, protested. She screamed, *"My father, Poseidon, will punish you for this violation of the laws of life and death. He will tear your limbs from your body and search for your dead relatives."*

Bion ignored the tirade and waved her arm.

*"Be gone, nymph. The Gods have rescued this young child."*

Again Tu expanded her size in a threatening manner.

*"You are no God, Bion. You are less than human. You have no will. You are a fungus that owes its existence to another form."*

Bion seemed to shake and a light was emitted from her head. Her face contorted and her eyes became vacant. Then a very smooth baritone and mellow voice said, *"Bion, the Pythia does not stand across from you. This child is protected by me, the Goddess, Demeter. Now let go of my daughter or I will pry your existence from you!"*

Tu, in exaggerated frustration, created a wave to absorb the Goddess. The wave encompassed the Goddess and it seemed to evaporate as it touched her skin. As it dispersed, a smiled appeared on Demeter's face. She again spoke, *"You have no power over me, nymph. Save your vengeance for a creature that will shake in your presence, not a Goddess that ignores your feeble attempts."*

But behind the nymph a larger trident appeared, and from the water emerged the figure of her father, Poseidon. He wore a shining helmet and his beard reached down to the center of his chest. He raised his arm and pointed it at Demeter. But as his mouth began to open, a flash appeared from the sky, hitting the water that separated the two supreme beings. A cloud appeared over the area and a voice said, *"The fight between the Gods is over. There will be no more threats or discussion. The child will return with the Pythia and remain in the temple for the remainder of her life. To satisfy Poseidon's daughter, she will inherit the strength of the child's vision. The child will see the light of the sun for only one hour a day. The remainder of her vision will be for Tu. I have spoken and the decision is law."*

Immediately, all the Gods vanished and the nymph withdrew into the waters. When the father, Zeus, spoke, there was no questioning and no protest. Only Zeus' daughter, Athena, had been able to stand up to and resist his glory. Athena had defeated Poseidon in the fight for Athens and had vanquished the Furies. Of all the Gods, she alone had the strength and power to supplant her father. Other Gods retreated in the face of Zeus' power, accepting his dominion.

Bion lifted Lasiandra out of the water. She held her as a mother would cuddle a child. Lasiandra's head had changed by the conflict. Her eyes no longer had their pupils. They were replaced by a blue jelly like substance. Lasiandra clearly was confused and disoriented as she was led away from the river, barely able to sustain her own weight. But she quickly realized that she was blind. Her pupils would return for only one hour a day.

The King of Kings was sleeping restfully in the garden. It was the first peaceful time he had in a long while. He arose and was immediately surrounded by five slaves. Wherever he went the King was pampered. On this day he was hand washed and oiled and his hardened muscles gleamed in the early light. As he was sponged down, the King kept a placid, expressionless face. It was as if his thoughts were miles from the bathing place.

One of the slaves reported that a very prominent and wealthy member of the Persian community was waiting to see him. The man's name was Phytalamus. Phytalamus had supported Xerxes' father, Darius, and was just as supportive of Xerxes. It took almost an hour for Xerxes to prepare his wardrobe and makeup before seeing Phytalamus. Finally, the Persian trader entered the King's chamber and bowed.

*"My King, I would like to donate to your campaign. I am too old to fight for your army, but I would like to provide you with gold to make your preparations easier."*

Xerxes looked sternly at the bowed man and went over to help him rise from the floor.

*"My friend, you have always been a great support for my family. How much money would you like to donate?"*

Phytalamus hugged the King and said, *"I have a million gold pieces that you can have for your army."*

Xerxes was impressed by the gesture, and after a minute turned to the slave in the corner of the room and said, *"This man's name is Phytalamus. He is to receive 8000 gold pieces from the army store for his generous offer. We are not to take any of his gold!"*

Xerxes turned to Phytalamus and said, *"Your generosity, my friend, is beyond my expectations. It warms my heart to know that you have such faith in me."*

The two hugged again and Phytalamus said, *"My King, I do have a request for your consideration."*

*"What is this request, my friend?"*

*"You know, my King, that I have four sons. They are all in the army and will march with you to destroy the Greeks."*

Xerxes began pacing and looked again at Phytalamus. He nodded his head. Phytalamus continued, *"My lord, I ask that you release my oldest son, Chancony, from service."*

The King thought for a moment and said, *"Chancony..... he is a lieutenant in the Immortals, is he not?*

*"Yes, lord, he is. He* accompanied *the army to Egypt and received acclaim for his bravery."*

*You should be proud of your son, Phytalamus. But explain to me, why should I release such an important member of the service.*

Phytalamus bowed his head and said, *"I am old my lord. My body is in decay. I need one of my sons to stay home and help take care of me and the work that I do."*

Xerxes was enraged but stoic in his demeanor. He looked at Phytalamus and said, *"I will grant your wish. But before you go, does your son know of your request?"*

*"Yes, lord"*

Xerxes turned and pointed to the door.

*"I will release him. Now leave me."*

Phytalamus bowed again as he backed out of the room. When he left, the King looked at the slave and said, *"Have Chancony discharged from the army. I then want him executed by being sliced down the middle of his body. I want one half of his body placed inside the entrance to the city, and the other half placed outside the city. I want all the army to have to march past both halves of this traitor. I want all to know that I will not tolerate cowards in my army."*

The slave bowed and left the room.

Xerxes was distracted by the upcoming invasion of Greece. The venture held many arduous and complex difficulties, not the least of which, was getting the army and navy to the battlefield. Xerxes army consisted of conscripts from over 45 separate countries and races. His army was immense; probably the largest and most well equipped army ever assembled. The infantry numbered between 300,000 and 500,000 men, but there were over 1600 miles to travel. There were six grand marshals, all of whom led approximately 60,000 men each. For this battle, only four of the marshals were accompanying the great King. The remainder of the men would stay behind and defend the empire. And these monumental numbers did not include the navy. There were over 1200 triremes. Nine separate countries contributed to the navy, including over 300 war vessels from Phoenicia, considered by most to be the finest sailors in the world. This was truly an epic undertaking and a devastating destructive force.

Xerxes' hair was now long and it took quite a long time for the slave girls to tie it in a tight knot. Xerxes sat naked as the task was completed. He was then dressed in undergarments and a tight, short dress. His upper body always remained bare, unless he was on a military campaign. Xerxes, the son of Darius, was very proud of his muscled body. He enjoyed it when slaves stroked his tight abdominal muscles. Finally, the jewelry was placed on his arms and legs, shining brightly and reflecting the incoming sun. He was an imposing figure.

Secretly, Xerxes was still angry at Phytalamus. Imagine, he thought to himself. How could such a man not understand how he felt about his army and the importance of the invasion of Greece? Did he not understand that Xerxes' feelings were paramount over all? Did he not fathom that the King of Kings stood just below the Great God? Did he not realize that all decisions emanated from God and fused into the mind of the King of Kings, that the King of Kings was the chalice by which the Great God let his feelings known!!!

Xerxes had to put his internal feelings aside no matter how paramount, as he had a very busy day planned. The empire was in the final phases of preparation to bring the army to settle the conflict with the Greeks. Advanced units had been leaving for almost two weeks. The army was so vast that it moved like a great snake, spread out over miles and miles. Some parts of units had already reached the Hellespont to prepare the army for the crossing from Asia to Europe. The road to the crossing was arduous as well. Elam, Babylonia, Assyria, Cilicia, Phrygia, and Lydia all had to be crossed. The crossing of the Hellespont itself was to be an undertaking never before accomplished in human history. The distance of over a mile of fast running water had never been breached before by such a large group of men, carts and animals. The crossing would save the Persians months of marching to circumvent it. Xerxes' engineers had figured an ingenious solution to the problem. Older ships were rumored to be tied together with great cables forming a pontoon bridge that connected the two great continents. This engineering feat would save the great King from having to take the northern route around the Black Sea. Such a detour would take many months to achieve and would delay the invasion by untold days. The Hellespont had to be transversed for this war to be successful. The Greeks would be a difficult enemy without diversion, but this large Persian hoard would only be weakened with any long delays.

The second great engineering feat that the King of Kings had commissioned was the building of a canal to avoid the rough waters surrounding Mount Ethos. 20,000 Persian lives had been lost when the fleet got stuck in the strait during a storm in their attack on Marathon. This ominous talisman was one of the forces that led to the Greek victory at Marathon. This man-made canal would allow his current fleet to avoid that danger. Xerxes was taking no chances. He wanted retribution, and revenge meant burning Athens to the ground and pissing on the remains.

As the King of Kings walked through the great marble halls of the palace, his thoughts drifted to the information that he had been receiving from the delegation that was sent to Delphi. He knew it was a long shot to expect that a negotiated settlement would be achieved. He had been ambivalent from the beginning about sending people to Delphi. In his soul, he wanted blood revenge for the Ionian revolt (which Greece supported) and the military disaster at Marathon. And yet, he also had listened to the warning of his teacher Hamas:

*"Do not continue to fight a battle that has already been lost. Live in the present, not in the past."*

But the Athenians and Spartans had spit in his face by refusing to succumb to the Persian might. How dare they not see that God had given the Medes his divine blessing as the chosen ones. Xerxes was the Pharaoh of the most ancient and greatest civilization that ever inhabited the earth. The Persians ruled the holy city of Babylonia. He had destroyed the phony stature of the false deity of Babylonia, Del-Marduk. All civilizations had fallen under the Persian blanket, and now the obstinate Greeks, with their delusion of Demos, would be next in line. The God, Ahuramazda, had bestowed on Xerxes the holy mission to subjugate those who believed in the 'lie'. Those who believed in the 'lie' were those who didn't understand the balance of good and evil. They were 'daiva'- bad spirit. The Achaemenid family had the ancestral right to rule the known world. Ahuramazda decreed it.

Xerxes reached the Temple and fell to his knees, raising his eyes to the heavens. He proclaimed:

*"Great Ahuramazda, the creator of earth and all its life, bless our undertaking. Ahuramazda, who created peace for all, and made me Xerxes, King of Kings, King of all the Lands, an Archimedean and son of Aryan stock, raise my voice for your approval. The rebellious lands of Egypt and Babylonia rose against your greatness and I smote them for you. I have promised to destroy all idols of 'the lie'. I uprooted the cult of the Daevas, they shall not be praised. I swear it to you, Ahuramazda, the Greek deities will fall as the Egyptian ones did. They are insolent to propose this new thing they call Demos. It is the birth of an unholy allegiance, denying the true nature of things. They*

*propose that their judgment overrides that of God. Their impertinence must be punished."*

The King of Kings now prostrated himself in front of his God.

*"Ahuramazda, before my journey begins, I seek your grace and countenance. And I promise that before this is over, the world will bow to your greatness."*

Xerxes rose and kissed the golden ring that lay on his finger. It was the most solemn thing he could do to pledge his oath to his task. It was more than making a vow to one self, it was making a pledge with Ahuramazda. He then walked slowly and contemplatively across the palace, going to his grand-chamber. His mind was engrossed in many possibilities. The preparation for the war was certainly paramount, but other concerns also wrestled for time in the King's psyche. The turncoat priest occupied a fair amount of his brooding. He hated that renegade as much as he hated the Greeks. Yet he couldn't find the man. He was like the predatory arachnid scorpion, hiding in dark, obscure places. When Xerxes was a young adolescent he was actually bitten by a small red scorpion while out with some other boys climbing rocks. He recalled the pain and sickness of the event.

The wicked priest convoyed his thoughts to the point of infesting his dream states. Xerxes was plagued by a recurring nightmare about the dreaded Ningizzida. He would dream that he was in large open space. It was very cold and he had fallen onto the hard ground. He had difficulty raising himself up and he was crawling from rock to rock, digging his fingers into the rock-hard ground. He was freezing, and as he crawled he began feeling his flesh transform. Blisters and bumps appeared all over his body, and Xerxes would reach down and find his hand covered in his red blood. The winds hurled around him and somehow the ground was being taken away as his sense of solidarity began to dissolve. Xerxes could feel his mind and body becoming depleted to the point of extinction. He would watch his legs being dissolved into dust as he lay screaming and crying. The anger for the priest that occupied his very soul was revisited many times in the nightmare. Over and over the anger of his humiliation from the Babylonian ceremony in which Ningizzida knocked him unconscious in front of the stunned congregation plagued the dream, as his thoughts regressed to that past time, but amplified his pain and humiliation. And yet throughout this horror, the King heard vague laughter in the background. The amusement originating from the disgraced cleric himself. He could see, through the mist, Ningizzida laughing and pointing to him. In some of his dreams the priest would actually approach him and pull his arms from his body. Eventually the great monarch would wake with a start, feeling his heart pumping wildly and sweat pouring from his pores. His dreams were such that he almost feared going to sleep.

As he entered the grand ballroom, a smile appeared on the son of Darius' face. His emergence from the doorway was met by a loud roar. The huge female lioness, Sameron, let out an epic greeting for her master. The animal sprung up and met the King halfway to the throne. Putting its paws on the King's shoulders and standing up on her haunches, the full grown lioness made the King of Kings look like a child. Showing its canines, the animal was truly a majestic and imposing creature. Xerxes stroked Sameron's back, and as unlikely as it seemed, the animal let out a purr of contentment.

Standing off to the side stood five men. All of them were dressed to the hilt in fine tailored outfits. One could not mistakenly take these men for anything but military elite.

Although they were all in the same room, they didn't stand together in any type of formation. In fact it was obvious that these men didn't have much use for each other, with feelings bordering on contempt. There were 30 generals of the Persian army. These men were five of the six chief marshals, and they were all here to report to the man who ultimately controlled their destiny. Two of these men would not accompany the great King to Greece. Mardonius, the brother in law of Xerxes, was the ruler of the satrap of Egypt. He was the pharaoh's representative to the people. Megabyzus, the son of Zopyros, was the man who ruled Babylonia for the empire. Mardonius would accompany the King.

The three other marshals, Tritantaikhmes, son of Artabanos, Smerdomences, son of Otoanes, and Masistes, son of Darius and Atossa, would all accompany the troops to Greece. The eldest of these marshals, Tritantaikhmes, was one of Xerxes' father Darius most trusted generals. Although a man who earned his reputation as a fearless and brave warrior, Xerxes did not trust him to the extent that his father did. This trust was further eroded when Tritantaikhmes argued against the Greek invasion.

Masistes was a loyal soldier. He was hesitant, and always checked with the King before making military decisions.

As the great King approached, Smerdomences dropped to his knees. As he did, he took out a large blade and placed it under his own neck. This was his traditional greeting to the great King, symbolically offering his life in service. Besides the teacher, Hamas, Smerdomences was the foremost strategist in the empire. Another smile emerged on Xerxes' face as he made eye contact with Smerdomences. Ignoring the other men, he walked to Smerdomences and gently lifted him from his knees.

*"My friend, it is good to see you again."*

*"My king, my life is yours."*

*"Tell me what you know, Smerdomences."*

Rather than answer, the crafty Smerdomences bowed to the King and motioned for the other marshals to join them. Masistes was the first to answer.

*"Lord, we have very encouraging news from our operatives in Greece."*

Xerxes straightened at the words, looking at the marshal.

*"Most of the northern cities of Attica have already bowed to your greatness. As you already know, Trace, Macedonia, and Thessaly are already allies. We have already established these relationships. They are all prepared to welcome you and your army."*

Xerxes looked again at Smerdomences.

*"Lord, it is only Sparta, Athens and a few of their allies who are resisting the inevitable."*

Xerxes responded, *"It is good, my friend. If all the Greeks bowed to our greatness we would have no place to feed our swords or to extinguish our anger. When I am finished with the Greek civilization, the disgrace at Marathon will not be remembered by history."*

The King began raising his voice, and all the generals seemed to straighten their postures at the change in the King's tone.

*"But my anger at the Greek civilization is much deeper than Marathon."*

As he spoke, the King's anger began spiking as he banged his staff on the ground.

*"I asked for peace! I sent emissaries to the Greek cities and they were unceremoniously murdered. Thrown into ditches and horribly tortured. The Greeks are a self-righteous people, believing they are greater than others. I have promised my God that I will make sure that history understands the glory of the Persian Empire"*

He looked with ardor at every man standing in the room. Xerxes paced for a few heartbeats, then seemed to take a few deep breaths and calm his fervor. But as his emotions calmed, Xerxes appeared to shrink a couple of inches. He patted the general on the shoulder and then with a small smile said, *"I am glad to hear that our efforts in Syracuse have paid off."*

Smerdomences smiled then answered, *"We expected that it would cost us more to secure that alliance. It was a brilliant decision, lord, to suggest to Gelon that if he asked to lead the army, the Athenians would reject that option. You have vision beyond the horizons, my lord."*

Xerxes took a few steps away from the men and asked to no one in particular, *"What else did we promise?"*

*"Not much, lord. The pig, Gelon, was satisfied with the 50 female slaves that we offered besides the gold."*

Xerxes smiled to himself.

*"Cheap,"* the great King said out loud, *"Cheap,"* he repeated. *"A small price to pay to eliminate 25,000 troops from the defense of Greece."*

All four of the marshals nodded in agreement. Xerxes was now across the room. He began to pace and finally asked, *"Are you all prepared?"*

In unison, they all nodded in agreement. Xerxes turned with fire in his eyes to face these men directly.

*"Our destiny waits. I will not stand for failure. Failure and cowardice will be dealt with swiftly. Now, return to your troops."*

As the marshals turned and left, a young slave girl entered, deferentially bowing her head. She stood silently as they all walked by. None of them acknowledged her presence. Finally being alone with the King of Kings, the young woman turned slightly to face him. Although Xerxes was now facing away from her, the woman reverently dropped to one knee. The great King scowled, appearing to have misgivings as he began to pace. After what appeared to be an extended amount of time, Xerxes looked at the slave. He motioned and said, *"Rise."*

The slave girl rose unsteadily from her knee. She had heard about the King's famous temper and feared for her life. But, to her relief, the King kept his temper. Xerxes stared at her indicating that it was time for her to speak.

*"Lord, a man waits outside to speak with you."*

Xerxes flicked his arm, suggesting that the slave should leave and let the man enter. Demaratus slowly entered the room. He was regal in his appearance as he confidently strode toward the King of Kings. Halfway across the room he bowed in silence. Purposely, Xerxes turned towards the window. After a minute, he turned and walked toward the ex-Spartan King. He continued within an arm's length of Demaratus and stopped. Finally, in an angry tone, he said, *"Drop your weapons."*

With a surprised look, Demaratus stared at the King. Xerxes took another step forward and repeated his demand. *"Drop your weapons and go down on your knees in front of my presence."*

Demaratus hesitated for a moment then patiently reached for his sword and slowly raised it from his side. The tension in the room rose considerably and Sameron sensed the change in mood. There was uneasiness, as neither man was sure what the ex-Greek King would do with his sword, as the lioness rose from her lying position to her four feet. Although quiet, Sameron began showing her teeth and shaking her head. The two men's eyes were fixated on each other, and, for a second, Demaratus appeared to hesitate with the sword in his hand. Xerxes, in a daring fashion, stared the man down. Moving slowly as he drew the weapon, Demaratus threw the sword across the room. He then dropped to his knees in front of the great King. Xerxes walked over to retrieve the man's weapon and walked back to where the Greek sat.

*"I have decided that it is time to end your life."* Xerxes said.

Demaratus was motionless and silent, not reacting to the words he had just heard. Xerxes raised the weapon and held it imposingly over Demaratus' head. Almost in unison, Sameron let out a loud roar. With a stark and expressionless face, Xerxes stood in this position, looking at Demaratus for a reaction. Demaratus sat still as if stone. If one paid close attention, a small driblet of sweat did appear on the corner of his forehead. But his demeanor and his body language did not indicate either fear, or even concern. When no specific reaction emerged, the King of Kings lowered the weapon and motioned for the man to stand. Demaratus spoke, *"Have I offended you, lord?"*

Again pacing, Xerxes said, *"Rumors abound. The walls have suggested that you are in contact with your Spartan friends. Yes, I heard a very strange story about a blank tablet being delivered to the Spartan King, Leonidas."*

The King walked to the window again, but out of the corner of his eye kept watch on the Ex-Spartan King. Then, after waiting for Demaratus to digest the treasonous rumor, he continued.

*"It is said that you are trying to fight for both sides. How do you respond to this suggestion of sedition?"*

Demaratus swallowed and said, *"Lord, it wasn't long ago that I carried your flag triumphantly to squash the Egyptian rebels. I have met every challenge that you have asked of me. If you believe me disloyal, I will end my own life. But you yourself know that rumors are like the wind, you can feel their touch, but they have no substance."*

Xerxes started to pace again in front of Demaratus with his eyes searing like hot metal into the Spartan's soul. Even with his movement, he was fixated on the Spartan. Suddenly, Xerxes stopped his pacing and walked rapidly to where Demaratus stood. Again staring him down, and after a few heartbeats with each man focused on the other's eyes, the King of Kings said, *"If I find that the rumors are founded, your death will not be pleasant."*

*"No need, my King, to point out the obvious to me. If you suspect truth in these foul smelling winds, I will spill my own blood."*

Demaratus, now feeling more secure about his position, raised his voice as he again stared at the King with resentment.

*"Xerxes, son of Darius, whose line can be traced to Cyrus the Great and his father Cambyses I. You are God's representative on earth. All glory passes through you. You are the embodiment of the Achaemenid Khshassa. You are the Empire. I sought refuge in this empire because of my hatred for the rulers of my people. They stole my rightful succession as the leader of my people. I stand before you ready to lead part of your army to crush these confederates and return me to my rightful position, as King of Sparta."*

Xerxes seemed speechless at the short oration from the Spartan King.

Xerxes, looking at the ground, appeared to not know how to react. He did not trust the Spartan. He believed the spy that reported through channels about the tablet that was delivered to Leonidas. This placed him in a dilemma. Xerxes also knew that

Demaratus was one of his better generals. Simultaneously he had lost some of his respect for his Immortal troops after their less than stellar performance in Egypt. Part of him wanted to cut this man's arms off, yet something inside hesitated. Finally he decided to change the subject.

*"What are the Spartan warriors like?"*

Demaratus hesitated, still distracted by the King of Kings' possible lack of trust in his loyalty. He worried how Xerxes found out about the tablet. Who betrayed him? Did Xerxes really believe this rumor? Why did he keep him alive? Not being able to answer any of these thoughts, Demaratus quickly cleared his thoughts. After a few seconds, he began to respond, *"My King, the Spartans are the fiercest warriors in the known world. They do not fight for territory, they do not fight for women, they do not fight for gold, they do not fight for God, they fight for their honor and glory. They have no fear, Lord. They are encouraged by overwhelming odds against them."*

Xerxes bent his head with an inquisitive look toward Demaratus, and in a questioning manner asked, *"Do I understand that when facing our Immortals the Spartans will not retreat or surrender?"*

*"Lord, those are two words that would never be used by a Spartan warrior. The Spartan warrior is like a solid rock in the center of a stream. The water cannot dislodge it and its flow is changed by its presence."*

Xerxes appeared angered. He said, *"The Persian Immortals are the greatest fighter in this, or any Empire."*

Quickly, Demaratus had to decide whether to speak his mind or hold his tongue. His life could depend on the decision he made.

*"With no disrespect my Lord, you have never encountered the ferocity of the Spartan. They fight with skill and no fear. They will bleed but never die. They do not retreat."*

Xerxes smiled.

*"I have not known you to exaggerate, Demaratus."*

*"Lord, you have never fought the Spartan."*

Demaratus left the King's chamber and Xerxes walked to the window. As if talking to the sky, the King of King's said, *"Demaratus is a liar, and he knows I know it. I believe that he has sent secret messages to the Greeks. No matter what happens, that man will not return to the empire. He will die a horrible death. Oh great Ahuramazda, thank you for your grace. You have given me the strength to see through deception."*

The son of King Anaxandridas II of Sparta, and descendant from the great Heracles sat silently in his room. His thoughts were still transfixed on the Oracle's message to him. Not a man to search his feelings, Leonidas knew that he had no fear of death in his heart. But his thoughts simultaneously returned to the possible ruin of his beloved city, Sparta. He could not, and would not let that happen. He swore on his family and his sword to fight even after death itself, to secure the safety of his people and their way of life. He knew though, that his line of ancestors watched from their perch in the afterlife, and this worried him. At times he even let his mind wander to the impossible. Leonidas knew that Sparta had no walls. Its army was all it needed to protect the city, at least up until now. But this threat was overwhelming. Although the King had every belief in the strength of the Spartan army, he was also a realist. What he heard of the Persian was daunting, and now he had a warning from the God, Apollo. And the warning was clear and specific. It was not cloaked in innuendo, insinuation, nor written in a vague poetic fashion. Sparta was now at a historical crossroad, and the descendant of the great Heracles knew it, and was afraid to admit it, but it concerned him. Their freedom and very existence was now in jeopardy, and only Leonidas could dictate the course of history. The best course of action weighed heavily on his thoughts. He was the 17th. of the Agiad line and he pledged the course would not end here. Leonidas dropped to his knees and swore his promise to his ancestry. Sitting on his knees, with his head bowed and his arms over his face, Leonidas heard a rustle. His survival instincts immediately took over, and with catlike quickness he rose to his feet and drew his sword. He was already prepared to lunge, the familiar face of Diodotos registered in his mind. His arm and muscular stance immediately relaxed.

*"You should not approach me as such; you could easily lose your life."*

*"I am sorry, lord. My master sent me to give you this message. He had heard about the message you received from the Oracle and would like to meet you this evening. He proposes an out of the way Inn, five miles south of Delphi. The name of the inn is The Inhabitor. If you take the south road from the temple, two miles into it you will arrive at a fork in the road. Take the right path and continue. You will reach the Inn. The Inn is run by one of my master's benefactors, and will be a safe meeting place. He*

*suggests meeting after midnight. He bids me to warn you about people who might follow you when you leave this residence."*

Leonidas snorted at the advice and thought, *"I am one of the greatest warriors on this peninsula, and this peasant is warning me?"*

But he remained silent, throwing his arm up to gesture that the man leave.

It had begun to rain that evening, but the 17th of the Agiad line saw this as an advantage to his journey. He did not believe in sneaking around, and he vocally let his slaves know he was going for a ride. Leonidas hid from no man. He backed away from no threat, even walked into peril to prove his superiority. He wanted to entice visitors, he wanted to tempt those who wished him harm to follow, and meet their destiny. A half mile into his ride, he smiled to himself as he believed at least five men were following him.

*"Fools,"* he thought. *"They will all die this night."*

The son of King Anaxandridas II of Sparta, and descendant from the great Heracles, knew that he had to make his stand before the road forked. He pulled his horse behind a tree and waited. Not five minutes after he dismounted he could hear the walk of his pursuer's horses. He went into his offensive stance, preparing himself for the surge of blood lust. There were in fact, five horsemen, and Leonidas waited for the first four to pass. They were walking slowly, almost daring him to strike. In silence an arrow pierced the back of the neck of the last man, and as in slow motion he began falling from his mount. The others were slow to pick up the change and Leonidas quickly followed up by slashing the legs out of the back two horses. Now chaos ruled as the horses shrieked in pain and the two men went flying into the bush on the side of the road. Quickly reloading his bow, Leonidas ended the leader's life, and as the second man was drawing his bow, Leonidas shot an arrow into his face. By this time the two men who were thrown from their horses had recovered and were rushing at the King with their swords drawn. As the first man arrived, Leonidas fell to one knee and cut both of his legs off at the knees. The last man now faced the King. He held his sword up by his shoulder. Standing in ready, the Spartan King said in a Persian dialect, *"You have a choice of how you die this night. My choice would be to slowly cut pieces from your body while running my sword up your ass. Such a death is long and very painful."*

The man's eyes widened in surprise and his fear became noticeable. Leonidas continued, *"Drop your sword and you will have a quick release."*

The man hesitated and bowed his head, dropping his sword in front of him.

*"On your knees and put your hands on the ground,"* the Spartan King demanded, and the man complied. Leonidas took a step closer and spoke, *"Do you know my name?"*

*"I do lord, it is Leonidas. I understand you are a King of somewhere."*

*"And you are Persian, are you not?"*

*"I am lord."*

*"The man who sent you, his name!"*

The man swallowed hard and said, *"Hamas,"*

With little fanfare and no apparent warning, the man's head was released from his body by a blow from the sword of the King of Sparta. The Spartan King stood silently for a moment and returned to his hiding place. As he expected, a sixth man followed not long after the decapitation. As he approached the slaughter, his eyes widened. Realizing what had happened, he began turning his horse to flee. An arrow immediately punctured his neck and he grabbed at it as he fell to the ground. Not dead, the man tried crawling away from the scene, but the Spartan King placed his foot in the middle of his back. Again in Persian tongue Leonidas said, *"I hope you are content, for you died at the hands of the son of King Anaxandridas II. You may curse me with your ancestors."*

Leonidas quickly raised his sword and drove it through the man's back, severing his spinal cord. The man shook, and then lay still.

*"Now this is done. Persian pigs."*

It took a few minutes for the King's body to settle from the adrenaline rush. He stopped at a stream and washed his sword and tried to clean some of the blood from his uniform. After the fork in the road, Leonidas again pulled off the side of the road and waited almost a half hour to make sure that no others followed. None did. He continued on to the Inn in confidence.

Entering the Inn, the keeper approached him and said, *"You are expected, lord. The man waits is in the back room."*

Striding confidently, Leonidas followed the direction in which the Inn keeper had pointed. There was only one table in the center of the small back room. It was dingy, as if the air in the room was centuries old. Besides the musty air, the room smelled of mildew. Leonidas hesitated at the strong reek of the room. He stopped for a moment from the shock of the stench. His face wrinkled when he entered. Leonidas then noticed a disheveled beggar sitting at the lone table. Other than a second chair by the table there was no other furniture in the room. But after an initial surprise, Leonidas' recognized the spiritual leader of the Greek Demos, Themistocles. He reassumed his straighten stance and strode to the table. The Athenian stood to greet him. Leonidas looked at this rag tag man now facing him. The King smiled, and took the Athenian's jacket in his hand, and smiled at the Athenian politician.

*"I have heard rumors of the great Themistocles."*

He turned to the side, hiding his smile.

*"I have heard, that the great Themistocles was a political genius. I have heard that this man is leading a governmental transformation. I have heard that this man was as great as any King that led any empire on earth. And yet, what I didn't hear was that he dressed with such elegance."*

Themistocles in all his rags, stood and bowed his head in reverence to the Spartan monarch.

*"Let me assure you, t*he son of King Anaxandridas II of Sparta, *that you should not judge this man who stands before you either by his outfit, or for that matter by the rumors of his reputation."*

The Athenian smiled and said, *"Great King, our destinies bring us together."*

*"No Athenian, it is not destiny that drags us into this horrible room. It is tyranny. Tyranny of the most foul kind. We are here because a foreign power threatens our very existence."*

*"I assure you, lord, that I am aware of why we are here"*

He pointed to the chair across from his and beckoned the King to sit. Leonidas smiled and responded to the invitation. Once both men were seated, wine was brought to the table, and as the Innkeeper left, Themistocles called after him by name and said, *"Jonka, make sure we are not disturbed. If anything unusual occurs, ring the bell."*

The man nodded and disappeared from the room. Themistocles began the conversation.

*"I see by the stains on your clothes that you have not just been hunting chickens this night."*

Leonidas laughed and responded. *"You are wrong Athenian, they were all chickens, and easily fell under the butcher's knife."*

*"We have much to discuss, great King, for I hear that the Persian warlord, Xerxes, has already begun his march to subjugate our homelands."*

Leonidas stared at him and Themistocles continued. *"We have had our differences in the past great Spartan King. We follow different Gods and different philosophies. But they are our beliefs, Spartan, not Persian beliefs. Our roots all spring from the same tree, my Spartan friend."*

Leonidas nodded in agreement.

*"We must stand together, son of King Anaxandridas II of Sparta, and descendant from the great Heracles. We have no choice but to trust each other."*

Leonidas was taken aback by the way Themistocles identified him. He had not realized that Athenians understood Spartan history. But Leonidas smiled and put out his arm in agreement. Themistocles grabbed his arm in an elbow embrace and both men grinned at each other. Now it was Leonidas' turn to speak, *"I'm sure that you've heard the dire warning that the Oracle gave me."*

Themistocles nodded.

*"My friend, Eudox, is scheduled to meet with the Oracle on the morrow. I hope our message is more encouraging."*

Leonidas' posture immediately straightened, as the veins in his neck turned dark red and protruded sharply, betraying his passion. *"I don't care what the message says. The Spartans will fight these pigs until the last man's blood covers the ground. I hope I personally get to face this Xerxes. I hear he is a warrior, but he is not Spartan. I will feed him to the crows."*

*"My friend,"* Themistocles said, *"It is imperative that we coordinate and act in unison. My suggestion is that Leonidas, the greatest of warriors, lead the land army, while I, Themistocles will lead the navy."*

Leonidas sat opposite him nodding his head in agreement. Themistocles continued, *"My strategy is to lure the Persian into a sea battle at the island of Salamis. The harbor is perfect for surprise."*

After a minute, Leonidas responded. *"There is a pass along the Greek coast that provides the advantage for a small force that can hold its position against a larger invader. At this place, my Spartans will wear the Persian down. It is called the Pass at Thermopylae. The pass is bordered by the Ageon on one side and the mountains on the other. It is the most direct invasion route, and Xerxes will surely blunder into it. The Persian advance will be restricted by the size of the road, and Xerxes will not be able to outflank my men."*

Themistocles was impressed that Leonidas had already been thinking about the way to defeat an army over 100 times their size. Leonidas continued. *"We will meet the Persian farther north and fight a defensive battle, drawing them into the Thermopylae trap. They will follow us as easily as a baby reaches for his mother's teat. We will bleed the Persian at this pass, and my hope is that they show their true colors and retreat as they did at Marathon."*

Now it was Themistocles' turn to feel surprise, as the Spartans had not been at Marathon. Leonidas, noticing Themistocles surprise, commented, *"We might be different Athenian, but we are both Greek, and the blood that flows through our veins has the same primeval source. We will triumph."*

Leonidas froze for a second. One could see him swallow hard and his face stiffened. It was obvious that his mood had changed to one of contemplation. He now looked at the Athenian directly. Themistocles noticed a slight twitch in the King's right eye. It was very unusual for the King to express any emotion. Again he swallowed, then he said in a very subdued tone, *"Before this is over, we will bleed, my friend."*

Themistocles also became introspective. He bowed his head at the last comment of the Spartan King. There was no doubt in his mind, that the mission facing the Greek alliance was daunting. Themistocles had already decided that he could not shift his thoughts to the enormity of the upcoming war. He had to ignore such thoughts, block them from consciousness. After a number of moments he said, *"My friend, we had sent three spies to evaluate the strength of the Persian forces. Although only one returned, his message was that the Persian King had an underling show him in person the strength of the Persian force. The arrogance of the man. He wanted our man to see his army as a way of intimidating us. He did not care that he would report back to us the strength of the forces. In fact, he wanted him to!"*

Leonidas listened intensely as Themistocles reported the numbers that the returning spy had estimated. He sat stock still, not appearing surprised at the immensity of the army. Finally, he said, *"I too have received information of the Persian force. It came in a secret message from the disgraced King, Demaratus."*

Looking surprised Themistocles said, *"What is his purpose? Do you believe his information? "*

Leonidas thought for a moment and then responded, *"His numbers are not that different from what you just reported. As for his purpose, the only conclusion that I can reach is that he seeks to gain favor with us in case the Persians lose the invasion."*

*"A very dangerous risk by the ex-Spartan."*

Leonidas smiled and replied, *"Numbers are numbers. They mean nothing to the warrior. In any case, he is a traitor and a coward. He continues to show the true color of his heart. When we destroy the Persian, I will personally end his life. I will not listen to or give credence to such a man."*

After finishing his comment, Leonidas spit on the ground.

Themistocles sat in contemplation, as the task that lay in front of them was intimidating indeed. He leaned forward on his elbows and asked, *"Where do you go now, King?"*

Leonidas laughed.

*"Athenian, I am not the one dressed as a beggar and skulking around Delphi. "*

*"I see your point, King."*

Leonidas and Themistocles rose in unison. The men walked around the table, meeting in the middle and grabbed each other's shoulders.

*"My friend, your people and mine have often seen each other as in opposition for the heart of this small part of our world. This*

*competition must end here and now. No matter what our beliefs are, we both face the same danger. We must put our political and cultural differences aside to join for the common good, or our seed will be vanquished. This land which we both love, will again be controlled by others. We will become slaves in our own land. I myself, prefer death to such bondage,"* said Themistocles. His face was serious and somewhat forlorn. He looked as if he had left this world in favor of his own thoughts. But as quickly as he left, he returned with a smile for the Spartan King.

*"May the light of the Gods shine on you and the people of Sparta."*

Ever stoic, the Spartan King stared past his Athenian counterpart. His look was multifarious and the Athenian politician had difficulty reading the expression. A few heartbeats passed and the great Spartan King, said, *"I am sad, my fellow Greek. We have wasted many years in internal conflict, worried about our own simple lives, while a villainous threat grew beyond our borders. I am sickened by our lack of foresight."*

The Spartan now turned directly toward his Athenian counterpart with a soulful glare. His face contorted, and the Athenian thought he was about to cry. But his eyes remained dry as a stone, as he said, *"Themistocles, the father of the Demos, our time has come. We must now put aside our provincial struggles and turn our attention to the greater disease. The Gods have decreed that we must prove ourselves against this monster. I assure you, the Spartan's will not be wanting in this struggle."*

The Spartan King turned and left the Inn. Themistocles looked to the sky and said, *"Athena, your people need you now more than ever. We are on the brink of destruction. The forces that stand opposed to us are greater than we've ever faced. I pray you will look down upon us and tell us your guidance."*

Bubo circled high over the green eyed Goddess' head. The owl finally landed next to the Goddess on a wooden perch.

*"No, Bubo, I know what you want. I will not intervene in this struggle. I know our children are frightened, but they must shed their blood to protect their ideals. They have chosen this path, and it is on that path that they must walk."*

*The owl squawked in an agitated manner, ferociously flapping its wings.*

*"No, Bubo, I said that their fate is their fate. They have chosen this path. I do admit I am jealous of these brave people. They are making a stand in the face of an unmentionable force. But history is history. If I intervene, they will not learn, and they will not grow."*

Again the owl screeched.

*"No, Bubo it is different. When I stand up to my father, Zeus, I do so to provoke him and prove my strength. No, Bubo, I will not intervene."*

The Goddess hesitated and smiled at her confidant.

*"Well, at least I won't intervene a lot."*

After silently saying his prayer, Themistocles ordered more wine, as he would be spending the night drinking until he slept. It was one of the great man's weaknesses, this dependence on wine to calm his raging soul. His great mind needed release, it needed a buffer against the veracity of reality. In order to focus, he first needed to detach. It would be a long night.

Eudox was terrified. In all of his years of diplomacy, he dealt with rationality and logical negotiation. Well in truth, many negotiations had nothing to do with rationality, and to think of it, logic also was often absent. But what it was, was face to face discussion with humans. Yes, most negotiations were deceptive and sides were very manipulative, but Eudox had studied strategy and approach. He was familiar with it and comfortable within the boundaries of the negotiated combat. Eudox had certain rules that guided his approach. He always tried to understand the culture of the other negotiator. He found that the person's culture frequently dictated his methods. He also seemed able to tell whether the other person was negotiating honestly or was throwing smoke in his eyes. Eudox learned how to read the other person's posture. He would watch the physical reactions of the other individual and how they reacted to his proposals. He believed that others could not resist betraying their thoughts and beliefs by the slight movements of their face or body. The eyes were the key. He believed that watching a person's eyes betrayed and reflected their thoughts. He especially concentrated on watching the watering of his opponent's eyes.

This existence of the Oracle was beyond his understanding and it frightened him. Dealing with a God was not in his purview and stretched his comfort zone beyond its boundaries. The stories he had heard were legendary and it was difficult to deny the precision of the forecasts. Besides the extraordinary accuracy of the Oracle, it was also very philosophical. Over the years, the Oracle presented an attitude about life. It was more than a predictor of the future; it was a teacher of behavior. The Oracle had always supported the arts and competition. It was the Oracle which persuaded many of the cities of Greece to institute Olympic games. The most famous value that the Oracle presented was when the King of Sparta, Chilon, asked, *"What is best for mankind?"*

The Oracle responded, *"Know thyself."*

The Oracle also suggested that the key to life was temperance.

But even so, Eudox was anxious about facing this transcendent unknown. He had initially resisted the idea that he should present the question to the God, Apollo. Themistocles was unwilling to budge, and eventually Eudox reluctantly bowed to his decision. So here he stood; this was the day, he was going to go to the temple and meet the Pythia, and present the Athenian question to the God, Apollo.

Eudox felt the tension as he walked to the temple. He wore a special outfit that he had made specifically for this purpose. It was bright blue, as he had heard that this color was favored by Apollo. But his legs still shook as he was met by the two priests. Eudox knew that he was to be taken to the Kassotis to purify his body. This cleansing process also made him anxious, as he didn't like standing naked in front of others. Being washed by the three slave girls made Eudox blush, and his body appeared bright pink after the process. When he finally was able to don his robes again, his blood seemed to calm.

As Eudox was led up the stairs to the temple entrance, he noticed a table situated to specifically block the entrance to the inner sanctum. He quickly drank the potions that were placed in front of him and felt no immediate change. The drinks were sour to his taste, but were not that unpleasant. The wine seemed warm, and went down his throat in a smooth fashion. The priests moved closer to the Greek to help him if his stride faltered. As he walked, the Greek diplomat felt his head lighten and his walk became more circuitous. His gait worsened as he was led down the darkened hallway to the temple hearth.

The fire in the hearth danced and Eudox was mesmerized by the changing patterns. He stood transfixed, his mind drifting into a vacuum, and the priests eventually had to pull on his robe to direct him away from his frozen trance-like state. But even as he left, the radiance of the flame seemed to follow him. The flashing brilliance of the light surrounded his mind and flew at his head. Instantly, when the ambassador's legs buckled, and he required the priests to hold him up.

Finally, after what seemed like miles, Eudox reached the holy Laurel and reverently fell to his knees. The laurel was Apollo's holiest tree. Shot by one of cupid's arrows, Apollo fell in love with a water nymph named Daphne. He pursued her with great ardor, much to the chagrin of Daphne. Daphne pleaded with her father, Peneus, to rescue her from Apollo's advances. Peneus considered many different ways to free his daughter from the clutches of the love-sick God. But every approach he considered did not work to divert the passion of the God. Frustrated and confused, Peneus panicked and turned his daughter into the laurel tree. Still in lust for Peneus, and realizing he had lost her forever, Apollo declared the laurel tree hallowed so he could always be close to her. He demanded that the laurel be worn whenever a sporting event was held. He expanded his edict to include all artistic events as well. From that moment on, and for time immemorial, Apollo declared that the laurel should be seen as a symbol of victory.

But rather than pray, Eudox nodded off. Again the priests had to intervene and gently lift him off the ground. As they did, they looked at each other, rolling their eyes. The priests helped Eudox down the stairs, as his legs felt useless and were not responding to the directions of his thoughts. Even away from the fire, the flames mirrored his movements. As he reached the dark, murky waiting room, the priests planted him on the bench and he almost fell on the floor when they released their grip on him.

After an indeterminable amount of time, two priestesses arrived. They both wore short, white dresses and were surprisingly attractive. But Eudox could not focus on anything other than not falling asleep and attempting to stand on his own. The two women redirected the Greek toward the Omphalos. As Eudox stumbled on his way to the tripod, his vision kept playing tricks on him. He looked to the tripod, but it appeared as though a fog permeated the room. Was it a real fog or was his mind just dissolving in his thoughts. He couldn't clearly focus his eyes, and at times, he noticed the form of the Pythia on the tripod, whereas at other times he saw the seat empty. Then, as if the sound was emanating from every corner of the room, the Pythia began speaking, and yet Eudox did not see her mouth moving:

*"O Pitiful man, why do you come here? Fly to the ends of the earth, leave your houses and wheel shaped city. Everything will fall to ruin. Fire and Ares, God of war, destroy all. Many fortresses will be obliterated, not yours alone. Many temples will be devoured by fire, black blood dripping from their roofs, portending inevitable suffering. Leave this sanctuary and prepare yourselves with courage to meet misfortunes."*

Half unconscious, Eudox fell to his knees again and ended up lying on his side. He was looking up at the Pythia, his face wild-eyed in wonder. The thoughts raced through his mind, but he couldn't give voice to any of them as they were random and disorganized. At one point he could hear himself yelling but no sound was heard. His thoughts screamed in protest. *"I haven't asked any question. The God doesn't know what we want. How could Apollo answer without hearing the question."* Unconsciousness and blackness quickly followed.

Eudox awoke hours later. He was sweating and he rose dripping in perspiration. There were two slaves sitting by his bed. As he opened his eyes, one of the slaves rose and quickly left the room. Trying to clear his head, Eudox noticed Philokrates hurrying into the room with the slave. He approached the bed and in a panicky voice said, *"Thank the Gods. Are you all right, Eudox? We were all worried about you."*

Eyes wide, Eudox looked up at the Thespian. He smiled when he realized he was not dreaming. During his unconscious state, Eudox found his dreams drifting through very scary places. He dreamt he was being chased by people who held fire sticks. Eventually they surrounded him, and he felt his arms and legs burning into dust. As the fire climbed up his lower body, Eudox awoke from his nightmare. Observing his friend's confused expression, the Thespian waited another minute until Eudox reoriented himself. Finally, in an excited manner, Philokrates asked, *"So what did the Oracle say, we have no information?"*

*"It was not good, but my memory is blurred. I only remember parts of the incident. I can't tell what was real and what was my imagination. They give you strong potions Philokrates."*

Philokrates stared at his Athenian friend in confusion. *"If you don't remember the words, what can we do?"*

Eudox recalled that he was told that a priest from the temple would be coming to explain what Apollo said. Eudox looked up at Philokrates and said, *"My friend, we must now wait for the temple priest to come and recount the prophecy,"*

Eudox replied, as the blood drained from the Thespian's face. Eudox then sat up, and to the best of his memory, repeated the Oracle's ominous warning. But, Eudox' memory was sketchy. He said, *"What I remember, Philokrates, is more the feeling of the response to what the Pythia said, not so much the words."* The two men sat with desperation pouring sweat off their bodies. Spontaneously, tears welled up in the Athenian's eyes as he struggled against crying. It was an out of worldly experience. Emotionally he knew that the message was not positive, but he couldn't recall the words or the exact meaning.

Two hours later a priest from the temple arrived at the Greek residence. Both Eudox and Philokrates were jumping out of their skin, waiting for the specifics of the message from the God. The priest was a tall, very thin individual. His face was shaped in an unusual fashion. His nose appeared too large for the rest of his facial features, as if it were pasted on. He also had very large dark and bushy eyebrows. As he entered the abode, he bowed to Eudox and Philokrates. He said, *"My name is Agapenos. I am here to relate to you what the God, Apollo, said."* Agapenos then slowly walked to a chair, ramping up the anxiety and tension in the room. Both Eudox and Philokrates were propped on their chairs, as if they were going to attack the priest. Finally Agapenos said, *"Apollo was very kind to you, respected Eudox. He did not wait to hear your question, for he fears for Greece. Apollo recommends that all Greeks should withdraw in the face of the Persian invasion."* Apollo further warned, *"Everything will fall to ruin. Fire and Ares, God of war, destroy all. Many fortresses will be obliterated, not yours alone. Many temples will be devoured by fire, black blood dripping from their roofs, portending inevitable suffering. Leave this sanctuary and prepare yourselves with courage, to meet misfortunes."*

Eudox looked at Philokrates. Both men seemed stunned at the recounting. What made the comments more ominous was that the priest repeated the warning with a droning flat voice. After the priest left, Eudox and Philokrates stared at each other for an indeterminate amount of time. Neither man knew what to say to the other. Finally, Eudox said, *"I cannot tell this to Themistocles!"*

The midst covered the clouds and the mountains. There was no sound except for the wings of Bubo circling overhead. The owl screeched as if issuing a warning to the mountain. Her mistress was angry and there would hell to pay to satisfy her mood. When angry, Athena had been known to become very revengeful. Once, in the past, Athena went into a rage and ended up burning many acres of forest to satisfy her lust. This time, her anger flew from her eyes. Green glow emanated from her eye sockets, as the light jumped into the clouds. It hit the higher clouds and exploded into a barrage of shadowy colors. Standing on the top of a large rock, the Goddess shrieked at the top of her lungs.

*"Why did you lie?"*

Athena screamed, and the vapor radiated through her back and outward through her mouth. She continued her rant.

*"I demand that your message better convey the future."*

Far away, yet sitting next to her, Apollo sat with a smug look on his face. The Goddess did not appreciate his look and his posture, and she quickly halved the distance between them. Apollo sat still glaring at her. An agitated calm appeared to replace the anger of the great Goddess and she stared infuriated at her fellow deity.

*"Do you understand the danger you have placed yourself in?"*

Apollo looked surprised. Through the millenniums he had never been threatened this directly before. And to add to the dilemma, this Goddess, who stood opposite him, was the arguably the most powerful deity on this mountain. She had often challenged her father, Zeus, and a few times forced him to back down. This, then, was not an idle threat, and Apollo sensed the hazard he had created. He immediately changed his demeanor. More humbled, Apollo finally spoke, *"Why are you so angry? This is my temple, not yours. I reign supreme here. They ask not of you, they ask of me. These humans want my guidance and direction. You have your manner, I have mine"*

Athena let the comments pass. She continued to approach Apollo. Then, as Bubo landed on her shoulder, she said, *"You will receive the Athenians again and give them a more accurate reflection of what the future holds."*

Silence followed, as the two deities stared into the soul of the other. The timeline disappeared, but the green glow never vanished from the eyes of the Goddess. The radiance pulsed with varying agitation. Finally, without argument, the God of mount

Parnassus, overlooking the Pleistos Valley, knew he was bested. With the slightest of movements, barely perceptive to anyone but the eyes of a Goddess, Apollo bowed his head in ascension.

# Chapter V- The Red Ground

It was late into the night, but the sky was clear and stars seemed to sparkle everywhere. The son of King Anaxandridas II of Sparta, and descendant from the great Heracles was covered with sweat. He had just spent the last two hours practicing his sword play. He had killed a warrior slave during the jousting and his heart was still beating heavily from the combat. He walked slowly down the path, his muscles still aching from the exertion. His mind continued to return to the warning that the Oracle had given him not two days previously. It was only during the sword interplay that Leonidas was able to clear his mind. Fear was not part of his thought processes, but his strategic mind was continually processing possibilities. Leonidas had total faith in his army and the ability of the land forces to resist and eventually defeat the Persian horde. Where would they make their stands and where would they have to retreat to? All these questions cascaded through his thoughts. He barely noticed the surroundings and a few times he stopped to complete his reflections. But then a sound of rustling leaves interrupted his concentration. Leonidas quickly regained his composure and readied himself. He was alone in this small glen, but such isolation did not even raise a brief thought in the King's mind.

Leonidas noticed three men step forward, emerging from the undergrowth to his right. The man in the center, clearly the leader, was immediately covered by the two others as they stepped in front of him. They were brandishing their swords and stood in front of the leader. Leonidas stopped and assumed his defensive stance as they approached. The leader of the three began to speak, *"What is your name, Greek?"*

Looking irritated, Leonidas said: *"If you continue to block my path, my name for you is death."*

Leonidas stood silent for a moment, then spoke again, *"Why must I answer to interlopers who feel the need to have three approach one? By your poor Greek and your outfits, you must be Persian. I am not shocked by your cowardice. Let the others step out from behind the trees and face me as well."*

One figure emerged from behind a big tree to the left of the King. To his surprise a tall, statuesque woman dressed in leather stepped into the light. Leonidas snorted and his gaze returned to the men in front of him. He slowly raised his sword and pointed at the Persian leader.

*"What is your name, scum?"*

The Persian smiled and said, *"My name is Hamas and we are visiting your putrid country. The great King of Kings will soon visit you and Greek blood will fertilize this ground. "*

Leonidas snorted again and made no movement. Finally he spoke, *"Hamas! I know this name. You are right Hamas, the land will turn red with blood, but I guarantee you Persians will return to your putrid empire without your heads. Hamas you are a famous Persian general. But I recall a coward who sends others to do his work. Am I not correct? And now you bring a woman to defend your honor?"*

Hamas laughed at the rebuff and then responded, *"And I know who you are. You are the false Spartan King, Leonidas."*

*"False?"* Leonidas asked.

*"False, yes. The real Spartan King, Demaratus, fights for the great Persian King."*

*"Surely you are not so stupid that you mistake a traitor for a King?"*

Leonidas said smiling. The Spartan continued, *"You will regret this day, Persian."*

*"And you, my friend, will be the first Greek to pay the blood price for your insolence. I advise you to lay your sword on the ground and accept your fate."*

The two warriors standing in front of the Persian general began to menacingly move forward. They hadn't taken a step closer to the King when a blade seemed to appear in one of the men's throat. He grabbed to his neck and the warrior to his left quickly glanced at his compatriot. That quick glance would cost him his life. Leonidas swung his sword, but somehow, by instinct, the man was able to block the stroke. But the force made him stumble backwards. Losing his balance the King stepped forward and immediately cut his right hand off. As the soldier lost his balance and screamed in pain, the Spartan King ended his life with a forward thrust into his chest. The warrior fell limply to his knees; Leonidas then pushed him with his foot to dislodge his sword. It was covered in red and the King took two steps backward. He looked up and spoke, *"Do you still want me to lay my sword down, Persian? You don't appear as confident now that it is a more even fight."*

*"You will die this day, Spartan. I hope you have made peace with your God."*

It was now Hamas' time to smile, and he pulled his sword from his side and moved forward toward the Spartan King.

*"Now we will see, Spartan, what skill you have."*

Stepping forward, Hamas made two thrusts, both of which were blocked by the Spartan King. Leonidas swung at his head, trying for a quick ending to the duel. Hamas dropped to his knee, the blade passing over his head. The Persian then swung at the Spartan's leg, hoping to disable him. Recovering quickly, Leonidas blocked the low stroke, quickly dropping his sword to meet the Persian blade. This was followed by six quick strokes in succession from both sides, as the metal clinked from the force of the blows and sparks seemed to arise from the contact. The two men backed up after this interchange to regroup from this initial parry.

Now it was the Spartan King's turned to advance offensively. He struck hard at the teacher's right arm, and then after Hamas' defensive block, he struck hard at his chest. In a move that the Spartan had never seen, the Persian threw his body horizontally over the thrusting sword, landing on his feet to the left of the Spartan. But with no hesitation, the Persian brought his sword up and thrust it at the King's hip. Although able to deflect the blow, the Persian's sword drew blood from the King's left hip. The Spartan stepped backward and with his left hand reached down to the wound. When it came up red, the Spartan King put it up to his mouth and tasted his own blood. A smile rose on his face.

*"Take joy in your brief victory Persian, for it will be your last."*

Hamas seemed to relax a moment, but surprisingly, the Spartan swung in a circle and cut the Persian's left arm. Stunned, Hamas barely recovered in time to impede the next stroke. But again, Persian blood was drawn. Sensing the advantage, the Leonidas quickly advanced and caught Hamas off guard. He pushed him down with his arms, and as he fell backward, he flung his sword into his unguarded chest. As the teacher landed on the ground, blood appeared from his mouth and his eyes disappeared in his skull. The Persian teacher was dead.

As the Spartan King reached down to retrieve his weapon the woman approached and quickly laid her sword menacingly on the King's neck. Immediately freezing, Leonidas looked at his adversary. With a smile on her face, the Warrior Queen backed off, removing her sword from his neck, and motioned for

Leonidas to retrieve his weapon. In very broken Greek, Artemisia said, *"Too easy, Spartan. To relieve you of your life would be too easy for me. I will allow you to live. But I warn you, such mercy will not be shown again. The next time you encounter Persians will be your last days."*

After she straightened up, Artemisia walked over to the fallen Persian and placed her hand over his face. Realizing that the battle was over, Leonidas allowed the Queen to pass unimpeded in reverence to her fallen friend. Artemisia placed her weapon on the ground. She looked up to the sky and mouthed a quick prayer. And with that, the Warrior Queen quickly turned, rose, and disappeared into the woods.

It took three days of walking and riding through the back woods and roads to reach their destination. Ummanaldash was not in strong physical condition, and as the days went by his muscles ached and his breathing became more laborious. To the eunuch's surprise, Athens was not the destination that Lysim led him to. As they peered from a bluff above the Aegean, Ummanaldash was surprised to see what appeared like a new facility to build ships.

*"Where are we?"* he inquired. Lysim smiled and said, *"The new port of Piraeus."*

*"New port?"* he asked.

*"It is rumored,"* Lysim responded in a hushed voice, *"That the Athenians found a large vein of silver in the south of the country. With this they built this facility and have created a large navy of new Triremes."*

*"How many" "Not many in comparison to the Persian navy. Only about 250."*

With urgency, Ummanaldash said, *"We must return immediately to Delphi. I must give this message to the delegation. It is important information."*

Lysim asked, *"Wouldn't you like to get closer so we can see the ships more clearly?"*

*"No, no,* "Ummanaldash immediately responded as dread welled up in his body. On the clandestine journey to Piraeus, Ummanaldash was distracted by his fright and anxiety. Now that he saw the ship works he didn't need to press his luck any further. He felt his neck muscles tense and his mouth dried. He wanted to quickly return to safety. In truth, ever since Xerxes informed him he was going on the excursion he suffered with internal tremors. He didn't much like this role of being a spy. He wasn't cut out for it.

*"We have seen enough,"* he reiterated, *"It is time to return to Delphi."*

On the second night of their return journey, the two men were sitting around their campfire eating some meat they had purchased from a hunter they had met in the forest. They were discussing the implications of the things they had seen at Piraeus. Suddenly Ummanaldash looked up, and the two were surrounded by five figures, obviously men who lived harshly in the woods. The thoughts of the new Greek ships quickly vanished from Ummanaldash's thoughts in favor of what he perceived to be a more imminent threat.

*"What do you want from us?"* Ummanaldash asked in an almost pleading voice. He and Lysim both stood up.

*"We are here to relieve you of your gold."*

The largest man sneered at the men as he spoke. *"We have no gold!"* Ummanaldash protested. At that moment, Lysim took a step toward the eunuch and ripped open his robe. Tied in the back of his body were two heavy leather bags. Ummanaldash looked at Lysim in surprise. Lysim then hit the eunuch hard with a large stick and Ummanaldash fell to his knees. He was crying now in pain, as Lysim grabbed the bags and ripped them off of his body. Lysim stood and walked over to the largest of the highwaymen. He spoke to the large man.

*"There is enough here to feed all of our families for over a year."*

The man nodded his head, as he took the bags in his hand.

*"You've done a fine job, Lysim of Onsclo. Your family would be proud."*

Still surprised and in pain, Ummanaldash looked up at the six men. He tried to rise to his feet, but another one of the robbers smacked him with a large weapon over the neck. He fell again, this time lying flat on the ground.

*"And what should we do with this?"* the large man said turning to his friends. They all became very animated and began banging their feet and weapons on the ground.

*"Yes, yes"* the large men said.

*"But he is a guest in our fair land. I hear that the Persians are superior to us wretched Greeks."*

The men continued banging as they laughed at the comment. One on the end put his blade down and lifted the robe of the eunuch.

*"Superior?"* he joked, as he pointed between Ummanaldash's legs.

*"Are they all born without tools to satisfy their needs?"*

The men laughed louder.

*"And how do they piss? Do they raise their leg like a dog?"*

Again the laughter filled the air. The large man walked over to Ummanaldash and poked him with his blade.

*"Eunuch, my friends would like to see you piss!"*

Ummanaldash hesitated, and the man poked him again, this time with a more serious tone.

*"Would you prefer to bleed?"* he asked. Ummanaldash stood, and then squatted. A trickle of urine passed from his body to the ground. Laughter again filled the air.

*"Do all Persians piss like that?"* the large man inquired. Ummanaldash didn't know what to say. Becoming even more serious, the large man walked up to the quivering Persian.

*"Does your mouth work Persian? Down on your knees."*

He then walked over to Ummanaldash and pulled his robe open, revealing a large and partially stiff penis. He placed himself in front of Ummanaldash's mouth and looked in his eyes.

*"You have a choice, Persian. Either show me how well your mouth works, or die where you kneel."*

Slowly the eunuch leaned forward, swallowed hard and took the large organ into his mouth. All the men hooted in delight, watching the Persian work on the organ. In turn, each of the highwaymen took their turn in Ummanaldash's mouth. Twice he threw up from the amount of semen he was ingesting. After all were finished, the large man again stepped forward to the eunuch. He placed a noose like rope around his neck and again he spoke:

*"You now belong to us, Persian. We have never had a slave before, especially one with such a fine working mouth. We will decide later, whether you are worthy of life."* With that, he jerked on the rope and Ummanaldash choked but rose to his feet. The group led him away into the woods.

The two men skulked through the narrow streets of the city. They had only arrived two days earlier in Delphi and were unsure of where their target was. It was unusual for two Sand Dancers to work together on the same mission, but this was important enough to warrant such an extravagance. Barick-el-som was the leader of the two, being the eldest and having the most experience. He had heard that another Sand Dancer had been assigned to this mission but had previously failed. Almost an unheard-of event. There wasn't much information on the subject to be had, but Barick-el-som knew that the failure had occurred in Athens. Three days earlier Barick-el-som and his partner in this mission had met with Persian spies. These men had told them that their target was in Delphi but traveling in disguise.

*"A fortunate circumstance,"* He had thought at the time.

*"This meant that their target was not protected by many men, probably only a few. Having more than two or three guards would raise suspicion. And for some reason their target wanted to be unseen."*

The second Sand Dancer's name was Saarinen. Of course, neither name was the man's given name. When one became a Sand Dancer it was as a new birth, into a new order. Original names were shed like a snake sheds its skin. Saarinen was much younger than Barick-el-som and much less experienced. This was his first mission as he had recently finished his training in these black arts. After meeting with the two Persian spies, Barick-el-som had Saarinen end their lives. He wanted no slip ups and eliminating the spies was the safest way to insure silence. Saarinen was a serious young man and relished the first experience. He took care of the situation with quick efficiency. Barick-el-som was proud of his proficiency, as he clearly had learned his trade well.

The two men were now engaged in the most difficult part of their mission. They had to locate their target who was traveling disguised. Barick-el-som did have a lead. He had gained the trust of two beggars since arriving in the city. It wasn't trust that he had gained, more like financial loyalty. Flashing gold and silver coins always made one new friends. The beggars had reported that they had noticed a group of three new people living in one of the back alleys. They seemed to always travel together, and neither man had ever seen them before. Barick-el-som was assured in his mind that this must be his target. He now knew that their target had two guards with him. Although he took nothing for granted, he felt that the situation was perfect for a strike.

That evening Barick-el-som and Saarinen slowly approached the alley that they had been led to. There were in fact, three men sitting around a small fire oblivious to their presence. The Sand Dancers slowly made their way down the alley closely evaluating other possible traps. There were a few doorways, but no one was hiding in them. The three men were approached. In almost perfect Greek, Barick-el- som said, *"Greetings friends. May we warm ourselves by your fire."*

The man who looked up had a round face and a short beard.

*"You may,"* he said. After a few minutes of small talk, mostly about the Oracle and its powers to see the future, Barick-el som bowed and said, *"I am sorry. My friend, Eudocia, and myself have been sitting here and enjoying your hospitality and we haven't formally introduced ourselves to you."*

He stood and bowed again.

*"My name is Lysimachus. My friend, Eudocia, and I are from the far north, in Macedonia. We are pilgrims here hoping to speak with the great Oracle."*

Barick-el-som did not want to use Persian names, as it would raise alarm in these Greeks. The three men did not immediately speak and Barick-el-som sensed their worry. From their subtle movements of the Greeks the Sand Dancer was able to judge that the round-faced man was the leader of the trio and probably the man they were after. With a glance to Saarinen the two men drew their weapons and ended the lives of the two men flanking the leader. Pointing his bloodied sword at the third man, Barick-el-som said, *"Now, my friend, tell me your name."*

Again the man did not immediately respond. But from behind Saarinen a sound broke the quiet and Saarinen slumped forward. Another sound shattered the silence and a second arrow was protruding from the younger Sand Dancer's back. Blood began to flow from his mouth and he fell in a heap. Fearing the failure of the mission, Barick-el-som immediately drew his blade back to strike the Greek down, but an arm grabbed him in mid-flight, causing his stroke to miss horribly. Barick-el som was turned around from the momentum of the swing and he noticed five men standing behind him. Now off balance and falling forward, the man who had deflected his stroke flung him down to the ground and pulled out a large dagger. In one motion he cut the sword from the Sand Dancer's hand and had the knife on his windpipe. Barick-el-som looked up in shock at the man as he had not anticipated such a defense. The man who stood above him had a weather beaten face, but clear and intense eyes. His grip and strength were powerful, and he spoke to the Persian:

*"Do not move friend, or you will sacrifice your neck."*

His knee was firmly on the Sand Dancer's chest and two other men pointed pulled arrows at him as well. The Greek who had been the target of the attack walked forward and bent down to speak to Barick-el-som. In a quiet and controlled voice, he said, *"My name is Themistocles. I am the man you were pursuing. You have missed your opportunity again, Persian. You Sand Dancers are not very good at your craft, are you?"*

And with a nod, the Greek sitting on his chest cut Barick-el som's throat. A hissing noise rose from the Persian's neck as his eyes fell back in his head. The man rose off of him and faced Themistocles.

*"What would I do without you?"* the founder of the Demos said. He continued, *"It was a very fortunate day for me when I met you, Thantos. The Gods were truly smiling on me."*

The two men hugged each other, and Themistocles looked at his fallen friends and the two Persian assassins lying on the ground. He looked back at Thantos and said, *"Costly it is. The new order of the Demos will cost many souls. But our destiny will not be denied no matter what the cost."*

He patted Thantos on the back and the Greeks walked slowly out of the alley.

Eudox was still shaken from his encounter with the Pythia. He was surprised by his exaggerated reaction to the experience. He stayed isolated from everyone for several hours. Finally, after a time, the Greek diplomat asked his slaves to bring him nourishment. Eudox could not decide if the experience itself or the message the Oracle gave were at the root of his anxiety. He had just began drinking the sweet wine that was brought when another slave begged entrance into the room. Expecting more food, Eudox allowed him admission. The slave bowed and said, *"Master there is a man, a priest I think, waiting to see you"*

*"What?"* Eudox asked, as tension snaked through his bowels. Was there more to Apollo's message? Was there information that the first priest forgot? His anxiety pierced through his veins and his arms began shaking. He actually considered not allowing the priest entrance. But he knew that he had to relent. He finally waved his hand to allow entrance to the man. The priest entered and bent over in reverence with his hands laced together in front of his body. His head was almost completely covered with a blanket. He raised his head and said, *"Lord, I am sorry to have to return to your presence with this message."*

Eudox straightened his back and remained silent.

*"Lord, the Pythia requests that you return to the Oracle and receive another message from the God."*

*"Another message?"* Eudox inquired.

*"Yes, lord. It is quite unusual. In fact, I cannot recall when it has happened before."*

Eudox was stunned. Without thinking and riddled with fear, he responded impulsively, *"I cannot return to the Oracle. It is out of the question."*

The priest bowed again and said, *"Please, lord. It is very important. Please think on the subject and I will return in two hours to hear your response."*

*"You can return in two hours, but I must warn you, you will be disappointed,"* Eudox replied.

*"I have no intention of going through that ritual again. It terrified me the first time, and it took me days to recover."*

The priest bowed a third time and retreated. Now, his thoughts racing, Eudox put down his glass. He was finally recovering from the first experience and he was being asked to return. But as he sat in confusion, the slave girl entered again.

*"Master, another visitor has asked to speak with you."*

*"Is it that cursed priest again? I have seen enough of him for the rest of my life."*

*"No, lord, it is not the priest,"* said the slave girl.

*"I am tired and upset. I really do not want to be disturbed."*

*"It is a beggar, lord. I offered him some money, but he said he wanted to bless you in person."*

After a few minutes, again Eudox decided that he needed to stop being so rigid and see the beggar.

*"I suppose it will distract me from my concerns. Show him in."*

The slave girl left the room only to return a few seconds later with a man dressed in tattered clothes. His face was dark and dirtied. Even from across the room, Eudox could smell his odor. Still deep in thought, Eudox finally cleared his mind for a few seconds and said, *"I am very busy, my fellow. I cannot entertain you for long."*

The man bowed and said, *"My apology, lord, but I want to thank you for your beneficence. "*

*"Beneficence?"* Eudox thought. I know of only one man who uses such a word. He now refocused his vision on the beggar standing in front of him. As he did the man removed his hood and smiled at the Greek.

*"Are you really too busy to speak with an old friend?"*

*"Themistocles!!"* Eudox yelled with exuberance.

*"Quiet, quiet, my old friend. Not many know I am here."*

Eudox jumped out of his seat and his wine and food both ended up on the floor.

*"I am so happy to see you. You couldn't have come at a more propitious time. Have you heard about the message that the Oracle gave to me?"*

*"I have, "* Themistocles responded.

*"It is a dire response. I think Apollo must have read the future incorrectly"*

*"Frightening, "*

He looked at Themistocles. He face looked as if he were begging to hear something positive. The father of the Demos stared into the heavens with a faraway look. After a few moments he looked back at Eudox. His face did not smile, but he did have a reassuring look as he glanced back at Eudox. He put his hand on Eudox's shoulder and patted it.

*"You seem worried my friend."*

Now he smiled.

*"For all the years I have known you, my friend, you have always worried too much."*

Eudox looked surprised at the comment.

*"A worrier, you say! The God, Apollo has told us to flee. That is not worry my friend, that is a warning."*

Again Themistocles smiled. *"My friend, I have believed in the benevolence and the protection of the Gods my entire life. In our most trying time, the Gods will not abandon our cause."*

Again, with a peculiar look on his face, Eudox said, *"I have never been sure of the Gods, my friend. I have never known whether they could be trusted. Even after my experience at the temple, I still don't know if their message is real."*

He hesitated, swallowed deeply and continued talking, *"I have never been able to trust the Gods……but I always have been able to trust Themistocles!"*

The men smiled at each other. They approached each other and hugged.

*"They won't abandon us, my friend. Don't worry."*

Eudox now had tears in his eyes. Again, he looked at the father of the Demos with an imploring look.

*"The message that the Oracle had given to the Spartans was no less chilling."*

Themistocles placed his hand over his friend's shoulder in his typical fashion. Such a movement often meant that he had something important to say. Eudox knew that usually such a message was not pleasant and it would mean being asked to do something he was disinclined to do. The two men walked slowly around the room and Themistocles continued. *"I had a dream last night, Eudox. I think I was visited in my dream by the Goddess, Athena. In my dream, I was standing in a beautiful field of flowers. I could feel the sun on my body. All of a sudden I saw an owl fly overhead. The bird circled me and came to roost on my shoulder. It made funny sounds, but my mind knew what it was saying. "Return to the Oracle. The first message was unclear".*

He looked at his friend as they walked. He could feel the tension in his shoulders as he relayed his dream.

*"You are frightened, Eudox. I have never seen you have such feelings before. I've seen you concerned and frustrated, and even worried."*

*"I am frightened, my friend. The Oracle experience was overwhelming. I don't wish to experience it again."*

They continued to walk around the room and Themistocles patted the shoulder of his compatriot. He finally spoke again. *"Whenever I am frightened, my friend, I think of the Demos and the importance of this government experiment. History will record it as our time. The faith in our cause will give you strength beyond Hercules. "*

With his head slightly bent, Eudox responded, *"Just before you arrived a priest from the temple begged me to return to the Oracle. He said the first message was not complete. I hesitate to return to that inhuman experience."*

Themistocles smiled and patted Eudox' shoulder again. With a serious and a genuine look, Themistocles said, *"You will do the right thing. I have almost as much faith in your strength as I have in the Demos.*

Silence then filled the room as the men made two more rotations. Neither spoke as both were in deep thought.

The night was not an easy one. The father of the Greek Demos spent a long night dulled by his wine consumption. As always happened, he ended up naked on the floor, lying in his own vomit. His second in command spent a much different night. He tossed and turned and had difficulty putting more than a few hours of rest together. His dreams were plagued by vague images of fear and horror. He kept picturing black blood. It haunted his night. In the middle of the darkness he rose to urinate. As he stood by the outside wall, he knew that he had to return to the Oracle. Eudox knew he had no other choice. As he stood relieving himself, he turned and vomited on the ground. He would not return to sleep or rest.

The next morning at sunrise Eudox reluctantly, but without hesitation, returned with the priest to the temple. He went through the ritualistic ceremonies required before entering the inner sanctum. His thoughts were drenched in fearful anticipation. Many times he felt bile rising through his throat. Every time he fought it back and swallowed hard.

Eudox kneeled in front of the Pythia again. She seemed to be in an apoplectic frenzy, wailing her arms and legs, in what appeared like an unholy dance. Finally, in a deepened but oddly melodious voice, the Oracle spoke, *"Athena, the Pallas cannot appease Zeus in spite of devoted persuasion, entreaty, and prayer. Yet I shall make a second and unyielding prophecy. When all Attica shall be taken, Zeus will permit Athena a wooden wall. It alone will not be taken and will assist you and your children."*

It was difficult, but Eudox made an extended effort to remain as conscious as he could. He wanted to hear the forecast from the God's mouth. He wanted to remember the words, remember the tone. He struggled even to remain upright, no less to remember the words of the God. He tried repeating the message word for word, but the attempt was of little success. His mind wandered, and even with the attempt at repetition, he could not recall the message in its entirety. He seemed to perseverate on hearing the Goddess, Athena's, name. But then as he struggled, the Pythia began speaking again.

*"Do not await the approach of horsemen, nor await the arrival of foot soldiers from the continent. Turn your back and depart. A*

*day will come when you shall face them again. O divine Salamis, many offspring of men and women will perish, either at the time of sowing or at the time of reaping."*

And with that, the Pythia raised her hands and rays of light seemed to arise from her fingers. At this point, Eudox lost full consciousness.

Two hours later Eudox awoke with a start. He was no longer in the temple but was now lying in a bed in surroundings that seemed familiar. It took him a few minutes to focus his eyes. His head pounded and he feared that his temples were going to explode. But as he focused, he noticed his friend Themistocles standing above him. His mentor began to speak, *"You are so dramatic, my friend. Other people visit the Oracle and return with no fanfare. But not the great diplomat, Eudox!"*

His voice crackling, Eudox responded. *"Did you hear what the Oracle said?"*

*"Yes I did, yes I did. After you were brought back to this room, a priest from the temple followed and conveyed the message that Apollo gave you. I was waiting for you to wake to tell you that I am heading back to Athens to speak in front of the great assembly. There is much to be decided."*

Eudox sat up and placed a hand on his throbbing head. He was able to lift his head to look his friend in the eyes. He recalled the message clearly and asked, *"What does the comment mean, that Zeus will permit Athens a wooden wall?"*

*"I have thought in great length about this,"* Themistocles replied. He seemed to look in the distance, and appeared self-absorbed and detached. Finally, after a few heartbeats, the father of the Demos returned to the present and looked at Eudox. He smiled and said, *"That is why I need to return to Athens. Remember that I had a prophetic dream before you returned to the temple?"*

Eudox nodded. But Themistocles didn't leave immediately. He actually took a few steps away from his friend and then returned to his bedside. He bent down, and went to one knee. He put his hand on his head and leaned forward to speak to his friend. In a very quiet voice, he said, *"I have lied to you, my friend. My dream was more detailed than I reported."*

Themistocles again hesitated and his voice became even quieter. After a few heartbeats he said, *"My friend, I dreamt of ships, many ships. I believe that the battle for Athens will occur not on solid earth but on the Aegean. The Persians are land warriors. They depend on overwhelming numbers to overrun the enemies, my friend. I believe the wooden wall refers to our ships. It is the only conclusion that makes sense to me. We will meet the Persians in our element, not in theirs. We will destroy them in the Aegean. I think the God gave us a way to be triumphant."*

He patted Eudox on the chest.

*"Rest my friend. I will see you in Attica."*

And with that, the Greek father of the Demos rose from the bed and left the room.

The Warrior Queen was not tentative at all. She strode confidently to Apollo's temple. A priest had informed the Persians that the God would hear their question that morning. She was the last ranking member of the Persian delegation, so the task fell on her shoulders. Hamas had been murdered by the Spartan, and the eunuch, Ummanaldash, had disappeared with no trace. She cursed the bad luck. She didn't have any strong feelings about the two losses. Ummanaldash was a non-factor for her, but she mourned his loss more than Hamas. She knew that the murder of Hamas would outrage the Persian King. This suited her well, for it would cement his resolve to attack and destroy the Greeks. The death of the 'teacher', the man that Xerxes was as close to as any other living person, was now gone. The man that the Persian King depended on for advice and direction was murdered by a Spartan king. It was another insult and would stab the King of Kings in his heart. Hamas had been his teacher and guardian since he was a child. Losing this rock that he had leaned on would be a bitter pill to swallow. But it also meant that Xerxes would have to rely more on her for advice. Anyone who held the King's ear more than she did was a perceived threat to the Warrior Queen from Halicarnassus. Artemisia now believed there was no turning back. The King's heart would bleed from his loss and it would lead to the invasion that she desired.

Artemisia's Persian guard, Adon, was beside himself when he heard that he could not accompany her to the inner sanctum of

Apollo's temple. It resulted in a heated discussion between the Phoenician and the Queen of Halicarnassus.

*"I am in no danger, Adon. These are soft priests and slaves. They cannot jeopardize me."*

*"In any case,"* Adon said, *"You will carry a weapon?"*

*"I will,"* Artemisia replied. Adon bowed but replied. *"My Queen, my men and I will be waiting at the temple entrance. If need be, we will fight our way in to get you out."*

*"Surely, Adon, although I am not surprised by your overprotective attitude, I assure you it is a waste of your concern. Sometimes I think you forget with whom you speak. I am the greatest Warrior that lives."*

*"I have no doubt, my Queen. I have never underestimated your skill. But no matter how strong and brave a Warrior, you still can bleed"*

*"I fear not death, my friend. I believe that the Gods fear me."*

*"You are not afraid of the Greek God, Apollo?"*

Artemisia looked at her friend and bodyguard with a mocking smile. She then turned her head and spit on the ground. Then she hesitated and smiled again.

*"Do you have a dream Adon?"*

*"What, my Queen?"*

*"A dream, Adon, do you desire anything"*

*"Yes, my Lord, I desire to protect you!"*

The Queen shook her head, then continued.

*"For all my life, Adon, I have dreamed of many things. But the one vision that stands out is that one day I will battle a God."*

*"A God lord?"*

*"Yes, Adon, I wish to fight an immortal."*

*"A God, lord.... Surely, you could not win such a battle."*

Again the Queen smiled. Adon had never seen such a seductive smile on Artemisia's face before.

*"Maybe so, my friend, maybe so. But wouldn't it be splendid?"*

Excitedly, the Warrior Queen said, *"At the end of such a fight, the God would have to admit that she had faced the greatest Warrior that ever lived. That thought, Adon, that thought drives me on."*

*"I do not understand, my Queen. But be assured, even if you battle a God, I will be at your side"*

The Queen bowed, but in her heart she doubted that she would need any help within this temple.

But now, here she stood, at the precipice of the God's temple. As was the tradition, the Queen was met by the two priests. She watched them in stoic observance as they approached her from inside the compound. They sheepishly told her that she had to leave her weapons out of the temple itself. Artemisia gave a wry smile and turned to Adon, handing him her sword. One of the priests blushed shamelessly when the Queen was told she would have to bath in the Kassotis to cleanse herself. She nodded and followed the two men down a path leading to the holy water. After she took two steps, she turned to Adon who was waiting with a pained look upon his face, and gave a few hand gestures. She touched a number of parts of her face and body. The Phoenician bowed in response, indicating that he understood the directions.

Artemisia was led to an area beside the stream and told she would have to disrobe. Although not shy, the Queen told the men that she would take her clothes off behind a bush on the side of the river. They agreed and she walked to the area. When she was completely naked, she stepped out from behind the bush. Both of the priests gasped inaudibly at the splendor of this magnificent woman. She remained stone faced as she walked naked to the waters, stopping briefly by the priests so they could admire her. Three slave girls awaited her to bath and cleanse her body. Artemisia relished this washing, as the touch of these women seemed to excite her. She could feel herself getting moist as they ran their hands over her body. One of the slave girls was exceptionally comely and frequently made eye contact with the Queen. Artemisia did not divert her eyes but stared deeply into them. The slave smiled when this contact was achieved. The Queen felt herself shudder when the girl's gaze matched her own.

*"What is your name?"* the Queen asked

*"Agatha,"* the slave replied. The Warrior Queen summoned the priests to the water's edge and demanded, *"This girl will accompany me to the Oracle. She will serve to meet my needs."*

The priests quickly bowed submissively, accepting the arrangement.

As the Warrior Queen moved up the temple mount she approached the table with the ceremonial wines. Artemisia knew that there was more in these ceremonial jars than grapes. As she took the liquid into her mouth the priests reacted to a small sound. When they turned their heads, Artemisia silently spit the liquid on the ground. She was then led down the long darkened hall which ended at the hallowed laurel. She did bend to one knee when the sacred prayers were given by the priests. She was then led down the darkened stairs to the room in which she was to wait for the Pythia. She sat on the darkened bench and gently rubbed the leg of the slave girl, Agatha, sitting next to her. Her rub was gentle, and as she ran her nails gently over the girl's legs she could see goosebumps arise. As they waited, her hand gradually moved up the young woman's leg till it found her sensitive spot between her legs. She began rubbing more rhythmically and eventually she bent over and kissed the young slave. This muffled the gentle moaning of the young girl. After a few minutes, Agatha let out a muted cry as she reached orgasm from the Queen's touch. Artemisia smiled, satisfied that she had found a new toy to divert her attention. Finally, a young priestess entered the room and said it was time to enter the sanctum. The room was small, with only the tripod in sight. But she noticed that there was a mist in the room, a fog, and a very sweet odor. The surroundings took her back for a heartbeat. As she strode toward the tripod, a woman seemed to appear out of nowhere, emerging from the mist. The

Pythia spoke, *"What is the question that the daughter of Halicarnassus has to ask?"*

Artemisia took two steps forward and said, *"Great Apollo, I am here to present the greetings of the great King of Persia and the Pharaoh of Egypt, the almighty Xerxes. He asks to know the future of the Persian Empire?"*

The Pythia seemed to be thrown backwards by the question. It almost appeared as though she was having a seizure. She shook and whitish foam flowed from her mouth. She leaned forward and in a gruff voice, spoke, *"Riders of the desert, beware of the rain. Only scrub grows on the plain, flowers retreat to the fertile pastures. Children of Arshama and Vishtaspa head my warning. I speak to you, Khashayarshah; Ahuramazda will not protect you from what is to be."*

*"The waters from the sky replenish the ocean. The large snake dies at the hands of the poisoned frog. Beware, riders of the plain, the fire burns but it does not raise the house. Descendants of Elam, ride hard.* **Pray to the wind,** *for your fate rides in its sails."*

The Warrior Queen appeared fixated on the seizing Pythia. Her face distorted at the strange sight. The messenger of Apollo was writhing to the point that she was in jeopardy of falling off the holy tripod. Her eyes were now afire with light appearing to radiate in all directions. Her chest palpitated and liquid flowed from between her legs as she lost control over voluntary muscles.

The Pythia continued: *"The future is bountiful, but the last gasp will come from the chosen children. I warn you, Khashayarshah, pray to the wind."*

This scene was creating agitation for the Warrior Queen. Her mind raced and deleterious thoughts flooded her consciousness. She couldn't decide whether she was actually in the presence of the God, Apollo, or if this was some unsightly rouse, a play being constructed by people desiring to take advantage of her. Then suddenly, from beneath her robe, Artemisia produced a scabbard. In the background, Agatha bent her head and pulled her hair over her eyes. Artemisia had cleverly hidden the weapon in her clothes when she was being washed. As she removed it, the blade shone brightly in the light as it reflected off the surface towards the wall. The Pythia was still lurching in her hallucinogenic trance. With quiet deliberation, the Warrior Queen of Halicarnassus stepped forward toward the sacred tripod. For a few heartbeats she stared at this woman who was still entranced. Her eyes followed her hair, then evaluated her distorted face. The smell around the setting grew more penetrating.

The Queen hesitated for another moment, beginning to reach out to touch the Pythia, but stopped halfway to her. She inhaled through her nose as if preparing for a physical exertion. And then her face seemed to transmute, becoming gruesome and ghastly. Her right arm slowly rose, and for another instant she stood transfixed over the Pythia. Artemisia lunged forward and swung the knife, slashing Bion's throat. With her free arm, she grabbed the Pythia and pulled her off the tripod and threw her to the floor. Even in her frenzied state, Bion had instinctively placed her hand over her bleeding neck. Artemisia stood over her with a smile on her face. She leaned over and lowered herself to one knee watching the death throes of the Pythia. She struck again wanting to make sure that mortal life had left this courier from the Gods. The Warrior Queen bent over to place her face a few centimeters from the dying woman. Again her look distorted into an angry scowl.

*"Where is your God, Apollo, now?"*

She then lifted her head to the sky and screamed, *"Come down, Apollo. Stop hiding behind these women. Come down and confront me."*

She was only half surprised that nothing happened. The Warrior Queen looked around, and in a low voice said, *"I thought so."*

She lifted the knife again and with another thrust ended the life of the Pythia. Artemisia wiped the blade on the Pythia's robe and rose from the floor. She then kicked the dead corpse and spit in her face. She took a few steps backwards and looked toward the slave girl, Agatha, who was crying and now huddled in the corner of the room. With her right arm she grabbed Agatha and turned to run. The girl put up only slight resistance, although her sobbing and her screams seemed to vibrate off the temple walls.

With astonishment, an emotion that she had only felt a few times in her interminable existence, the green eyed Goddess watched the brutal event. Her eyes flashed in a changing perspective. They slowly squinted, as if she were evaluating this event. She could not fathom the unexpected horror of the event and the feelings of admiration she felt for this aggressive female mortal. Athena looked around trying to find Apollo to see his reaction, but he was nowhere to be found. Funny, she thought, such a direct insult, and yet he chooses not to respond. She knew that her power and influence were waning, and she wondered whether Apollo had either lost his ability or his interest in this outcome. It was perplexing to her as she debated the dilemma in her thoughts.

This was a talisman. History was evolving past her. She could sense it in her bones and on her skin. She could intervene, but some unknown force seemed to paralyze her. She watched this woman and the slave girl running through the temple and wondered how mortals could reach the point where they lost their fear of the Gods' retaliation. She never thought she would see such an event.

A tear appeared but she quickly wiped it from her face. Fate was fate and she pulled her gaze away from the event. But as she turned, she could hear the sound of distant thunder approaching below her. The sky had suddenly turned dark and a storm was threatening the temple below.

Outside of the temple, Adon stood with his legs apart and in a defensive position. He, too, heard the thunder and looked up at the darkening sky. The clouds were ominous and the wind had picked up. But he stood at the temple entrance, unwavering, daring the sky to strike him down. In the background, lightening flashed across sky, warning those not to challenge its superiority. But Adon stood facing the temple, ignoring the warnings from the sky. The rain began falling in torrents, but still he stood, waiting to see the woman who was more important to him than his own life.

The Phoenician guards heard a ruckus amidst the thundering sky. Their focus was away from the sky and centering on the temple itself. There were screams and a general sense of pandemonium arising from the inner sanctum. Adon, Artemisia's personal guardian, was very quick to react to the commotion. Three Greek hoplites also heard the commotion and began running through the pouring rain towards the temple. But in order to reach the entrance, they had to pass the large Phoenician blocking the entrance. His Queen was inside and something was happening. Although he did not know what had occurred, his instincts told him that his Queen was in trouble. The three Greek warriors were almost upon him and Adon had to either react or back off. Intuitively he stepped to block the entrance.

The leading Greek warrior shouted, *"Out of our way. There is trouble in the temple"*

Adon stood firm and when the man was almost in reach, he unleashed his sword. The Greek stopped in his tracks surprised by the Phoenician's action. It was in that split hesitation, that brief moment of indecision that cost him his life. Adon slashed his sword through the man's chest. The Greek, completely stunned by the action, looked down at his mortal wound. With his surprised face dripping from the pelting rain, and feeling the agonizing pain of life draining from his body, he looked at Adon with an astonished look and fell to the ground. Seeing the attack on their comrade, the other two Greek warriors raised their swords. After a second of hesitation, they charged.

Adon was not an easy man to be reckoned with. He had fought many battles in his lifetime and had vanquished fear from his mind many years before. His muscles tensed and he bent backwards to avoid a thrust from one of the Greek warriors who were now upon him. Even though the blow was mostly avoided, a gash appeared on his arm and began dripping blood. Without much trouble, the other two Greek warriors were quick to return to their ancestors.

While Adon was securing the front of the temple, the other three Phoenician warriors rushed to his side. Without words he pointed into the temple and the message was immediately read.

The other warriors rushed into the temple itself. They quickly dispersed three of the Oracle's priests who only half-heartedly offered resistance. Even though the priests quickly retreated from their positions, the Phoenicians gave quick chase and ended their lives. Halfway down the long hall they saw the Warrior Queen dragging the slave girl quickly approaching them. There was no questioning as Artemisia continued past the three men. They seemed to form a wall around the two women as they passed. By the time the five reached the outside of the building, Adon was standing triumphantly in a protective posture. His hands were on his hips as he faced away from the temple. Blood covered parts of his face and his tunic had red splashes upon it. The pounding rain mixed with the blood coming from his arm fell to the ground creating a small reddish puddle. As the five reached him, Adon lifted his sword and waved it over his head. He pointed to the sky acknowledging their triumph. When his eyes met Artemisia's their focus immediately changed to relief. Horses waited at an alley to the side of the temple. The six rode quickly and were seen leaving Delphi heading north.

After mounting, Artemisia pointed to Adon's arm which was still dripping blood. She shook her head at him signaling her surprise at the wound. Adon turned his face away obviously embarrassed by the wound. After a mile Adon yelled across to his Queen, *"What happened in there, my Queen?"*

With sarcasm, Artemisia said, *"The Pythia suddenly died."*

*"On her own?"* Adon inquired

*"She had some help from the Queen of Halicarnassus."* Artemisia said with a smile.

That evening the group rested in a dense forest in northern Greece. The guards had hunted and killed a deer that was roasting on the fire. The Queen sat on a log almost six feet from the fire. The rain had subsided two hours before and the sky was pleasant with a gentle breeze. Agatha sat near the Queen but appeared dazed by the experience. Adon approached the Queen and sat next to her on the log. For a few minutes he stared into the fire. Finally he asked, *"I am curious, my Queen, why did you kill the Pythia."* His question was met with silence. But then the Queen said, *"I'm really not sure, Adon."* The two sat in silence again for a period of time. Finally, Artemisia said in a soft tone: *"It is not what I expected, Adon"*

*"What do you mean, my Queen?"*

The Warrior Queen of Halicarnassus again sat silently for a few heartbeats, then said, *"Fighting with the God. It was not what I expected"*

*"What did you expect, my Queen?"*

*"A response, Adon, I expected a response!"*

The sun was setting on the plain outside of the ancient city. It was cooler than normal and the forest still held many large and thick-leafed trees. The man standing in the clearing had not seen his beloved Athens for years. As he stood, able to admire the outline of Athens, his eyes welled with tears. He had been summoned to this meeting place by a communication brought to him by an anonymous messenger in the night. At first he considered it a joke, a ruse being played on him by a revengeful enemy. All who knew him realized that his ostracism from his beloved city broke his heart more than any woman could have. Aristides went into a protracted depression when he was exiled from Athens.

Aristides had placed his political future in the hands of the Athenian populace in his perspicacious battle with Themistocles. The two politicians had battled for the hearts and souls of the Athenian Demos from its inception. Aristides was a member of the aristocracy and from the beginning of their debate did not believe that the Persian threat was real. He further had argued that Athens should not abandon their superior ground forces in favor of building ships and placing their future on an uncertain strategy. Aristides argued that the Greek hoplites were greatly outnumbered by the Persians at Marathon, and overcame the odds. There was no reason to believe the same would not now also be true, he reasoned. Although generally rejecting the concept of tyrannical government, the idea that the people should vote on policy scared Aristides. Yet he ultimately placed his fate in their hands and suggested an ostracism vote. When he lost to Themistocles, he was stunned.

When he left Athens, he entered a dark hole of despair. He had fought all his life for justice and decency, and for all his dedication he was banished from his city. It took him weeks before he could even recognize the light of day. He spent most of his time huddled in his bed, obsessively reviewing past events to try to determine what happened to his brilliant political career. He remembered word for word conversations with others and reviewed his responses in detail. For the first couple of weeks, Aristides slept for only a few hours on and off. His mind was starting to lose its cohesion.

And then one night, a message arrived that Aristides never thought he would see. It read:

*"The greatest peril that the Greek world has ever seen is upon us.*

*Your beloved city needs your service again.*

*All loyal Athenians need to return to the womb of their birth."*

The messenger then handed Aristides a map directing him to this rendezvous. Still not sure whether this was not just a plan devised by his enemies to embarrass and shame him, Aristides stood in the clearing, slowly pacing around the area. To his surprise a figure appeared out of the forest. Aristides 'The Just' immediately recognized the man by his walk. He took a few hesitant steps and Themistocles raised his hand in salute. The two political enemies had different feelings at this time. Themistocles knew that the people needed Aristides. After all, Aristides was one of the heroes of the battle of Marathon. He was an experienced general and his discipline and single mindedness made him an exceptional warrior and strategist. He was honestly happy to see that Aristides had responded to his message to return to the fold. Aristides, on the other hand, was filled with jubilation. The message was not phony, and he was wishing beyond hope that he could again walk the streets of his beloved city.

Themistocles approached the ostracized politician, and as he reached him, bent to one knee in front of Aristides. Noticing the little used greeting, Aristides also bent to one knee. Themistocles placed his right hand on the ground, spreading his fingers. Aristides copied the procedure and the two men locked hands.

Themistocles spoke, *"We both agree to put down our enmity here."*

Aristides nodded in agreement, tears freely flowing down his cheeks.

*"Our task, from this day forward, is to defeat the Persian."*

Both men rose and hugged. Aristides backed off, and even though he was silent, his soul celebrated his return. His damp face betrayed his true feelings.

The next day the crowd gathered early in anticipation of the debate. Gossip and fear were sweeping through the city like a wild fire burning dried grass. The populace was panicking as the horror of the invading Persian became more apparent. The rumors that spread through the city spoke of betrayal and surrender. But the populace was scared. Both of the Oracle's messages were widely known. Many people and politicians were frozen by the first message.

*"O pitiful man, why do you come here? Fly to the ends of the earth. Leave your houses and wheel-shaped city. Everything will fall to ruin. Fire and Ares God of war, destroy all. Many fortresses will be obliterated, not yours alone. Many temples will be devoured by fire, black blood dripping from their roofs, portending inevitable suffering. Leave this sanctuary and prepare yourselves with courage to meet misfortunes."*

There was a large portion of the population who believed that Athens should evacuate the city and flee as far as they could. Temple's devoured, black blood dripping from the roof. Such images shook the foundation of the culture. Probably the most powerful message from the first Oracle reading was the phrase, *"everything will fall to ruin"*. Even after the second message, many of the politicians couldn't get past this first prophecy. They argued that no matter what the second forecast implied, the first appeared very clear. Athens will be destroyed. Burned to the ground, obliterated. Usually the Oracle was vague or difficult to read, but this message was clearer than the most pristine lake.

Themistocles stood on the podium. A large majority of the male populace of Athens stood before him. In the beginning of this debate there was little decorum as men yelled out thoughts and fears at random. The tension and anxiety that flowed through the air was palpable. This scenario was the worst possible situation for a budding democracy. The city was teetering on the brink of chaos and the rational decision making that was envisioned for the Demos had been replaced by terror and dread. Finally, Themistocles raised his hands to silence the crowd. He spoke, *"My fellow Athenians. It is not time for panic. We have faced crisis before. It is time for strength. We must trust the Gods who have given us the fortitude to overcome this impending trouble. When the Persian attacked Marathon, the great general Miltiades did not run. Miltiades out thought the Persian. The Persians landed at the plain of Marathon and Miltiades positioned his troops so that the Persian rear was the great swamp. He then seduced the Persian general, Datis, to leave the battle with his cavalry. Miltiades took advantage and he took the initiative, surprising the Persians and they retreated into the swamp to their deaths. That is the Athenian spirit. We are all part of that victory at Marathon. It is in our blood to save our city, save our Demos, and more importantly, save our spirit."*

A man stood in the back of the assemblage. He spoke out.

*"The Oracle told us to build a wooden wall which will not be breached. If we are to build a wall around our city, we must start now!"* he bellowed. Many in the crowd rose and agreed with the man.

*"We waste time, we must start now to build"* another chimed in.

*"The wall must be built around the Acropolis and the temple of Athena. We must not let it be taken."*

*"Athena will protect us!"* another screamed.

As they spoke a cloud of anxiety seemed to overcome many of the people, with some even beginning to leave. Some men openly began weeping. All of a sudden a disturbance began to the left of the podium. A man arose and a buzz went through the assembled mass.

*"It is Aristides,"* a voice in the back yelled out. Another said, *"Aristides has returned. He will lead us against the Persians. He will tell us where to build the wall."*

The ostracized politician made his way to the podium. The arrival of Aristides seemed to energize the assemblage. Many stood and yelled in support at the return of a man who once was one of the most influential and powerful men in Athens. Aristides stepped up to the podium and raised his arms. A quiet swept the arena in anticipation of the message. Many sensed another political confrontation between Aristides and Themistocles. The two men had always been on the opposite side of issues, and many were expecting him to polarize the public opinion. He began to speak:

*"My fellow Athenians. Themistocles and I have fought many political battles in our time. You are all aware of our disagreements. But today you will not see dissention between us. We disagree on most theoretical political issues. But what we agree on is our love for Athens. We have agreed to put our issues aside and fight the Persians. For we must all stand together or we shall be overwhelmed by this enemy."*

The crowd seemed stunned as if disappointed in not hearing a quarrel between these two political heavyweights. Aristides spoke again.

*"Athenians! I have already spoken in detail with Themistocles. I urge you to listen to his plan to save our civilization."*

Again the crowd silenced. They all sat in anticipation of the plan.

Themistocles paced, waiting for complete quiet before speaking. He then allowed the anticipation to build. Finally he spoke.

*"This war will be different than any conflict we have ever faced. It will not only be for commerce, like our war with Aegina. This war is for survival, and thusly the strategy has to be more encompassing than just sending an army to meet the enemy. Every Athenian citizen will be asked to participate in defense of our beloved city and its Demos. Make no mistake, my fellow citizens,*

*this fight is about gaining freedom and self-determination or sinking back into the black earth of slavery.*"

Men began to yell, *"We will not submit to slavery. We will fight to the death before we will bow to the Persian."*

Themistocles continued.

*"Every man, every man will be enlisted into our new navy."*

An audible hush swept the assembly.

*"What will our families do if we all fight?"*

Again Themistocles raised his hands.

*"Our brothers in the city of Troezen have agreed to protect our woman and children while the men are in the navy. We will evacuate the entire city both to Troezen and the island of Salamis. Every able-bodied man will join the navy and man the triremes."*

Some in the crowd protested. A man to the right of the podium, and one of the generals of the Athenian cavalry, rose to protest.

*"We cannot abandon our land army or cavalry. Who will meet the Persian army?"*

Themistocles responded.

*"The Spartans and some of our allies will lead the land defense, while we and some of our other allies will lead the sea defense."*

A man arose, again to the right of the podium.

*"My name is Cimon. Most of you know me."*

Cimon had risen within the cavalry ranks as one of the most spectacular horsemen and bravest warriors. He strode slowly to the podium. He walked up to Themistocles and bowed. He then handed him his bridle and fell to one knee.

*"I offer my bridle to you to show my loyalty to Athens and our Demos. If you believe that our best chance is on the waves, then I will give up my horse in favor of the oar."*

He turned and many other men lined up, approaching the podium carrying their bridles to offer them in devotion to the cause.

Themistocles continued his argument.

*"My fellow Athenians, Zeus is permitting us a wooden wall. But the wall that Apollo is referring is not a wall on the earth. It is a wall of ships. A wall of wooden ships. We will take to the sea to defeat the Persian."*

A roar of agreement went up through the crowd. He continued, *"Apollo said, 'O Divine Salamis'. He did not say 'O Cursed Salamis'. We will make our play outside of Salamis."*

Again the crowd roared in concurrence. The decision had been made; the vote was an afterthought.

# Chapter VI- Pronouncement

It was surprising to her that she was not more depressed at the death of her friend. Lasiandra had adjusted more slowly being blind than she had expected. Initially the dark terrified her. She believed that her useful life was over with the loss of her sight. But now, after her adjustment, she realized that her blindness let her observe more than she could when she had sight. She had sacrificed her sight for pure vision. The blindness increased her meditation time and her relationship with Demeter grew. Many hours a day were spent in the world of contemplation, flying free through the clouds.

When Lasiandra heard of the death of her mentor, Bion, her first thoughts centered around revenge. In her thoughts she hunted Artemisia down, finally taking her life in a violent confrontation.

Although she knew such a reality was not possible, she found comfort in the fantasy.

As her lust for revenge, Lasiandra knew that the Gods had a plan. She believed in their love and their guidance. Although she reached rapture with her own deity, she was often confused by many of the events that were attributed to all of the deities. In this case, the disorganized nature of the event suggested to her a primordial hand.

Besides her contemplation practice, Lasiandra prayed to Apollo for understanding. Why would a God allow the murder of his messenger? Why would he not protect the person that had a connection to his own body? Bion was a preacher of love who died with violence, a situation that in her private thoughts made Lasiandra believe only for a second or two, that the God had abandoned his lamb in favor of chaos. Did he really understand what he had allowed to happen? Her answer was that, of course he did, he was a God. Lasiandra looked to the heavens and pleaded, *"Apollo, why have you forsaken your children? Have we sinned against you?"*

Lasiandra fell to her knees and sobbed uncontrollably.

Apollo did not answer her prayers, nor did Demeter. But one night, in the presence of a blood red moon, a vision appeared to the adolescent. Initially the vision was vague, and Lasiandra felt a surge of fear run through her veins. But as the vision stabilized, it convalesced into the image of an old woman, dressed in velvet rags. It was a strange sight for this blind child to see such an image. It was out of context with her lack of vision, but there it stood nonetheless. As the vision grew, Lasiandra began hearing sound emanating from someplace she couldn't identify. The old woman's mouth did not move but the sound congealed into words. As the sound grew more understandable, Lasiandra felt her muscles tighten and her heart begin to palpitate. Something was happening that was both terrifying and exciting at the same time. Lasiandra finally realized that she was in the presence of omnipotent power. It wasn't a conscious thought, but she could feel her bones and organs respond to the manifestation as if the force were pulling at her very existence. Every cell in her body was on fire, but the pain was transformed into unrecognizable pleasure. This was followed by a feeling of comfort, which she first thought was the beginning of death itself.

The woman reached out to the child as she approached. Lasiandra could not resist the invitation and she found herself drifting closer to the image. The sound now became more codified into a voice.

*"Do not mourn, my child. Your teacher is with me. She has earned her place in my realm. She has chosen to work with trees for the rest of his existence, and they will revel in her attention."*

The voice stopped as Lasiandra looked up at the mystical face. She instantly noticed the shining green eyes that encompassed the woman's face. The other facial features were almost unrecognizable in comparison to those shining lights. But even as she had heard the message, she did not notice the image speaking, but the words were appearing in her mind, transmuted from the image to her without the help of the air.

*"I come now to settle your spirit, little one. Don't think notice wasn't paid. The way of things is that death must precede rebirth. But to you, that rebirth might be unrecognizable. You believe in your mind that this brutal event marks the end, but in truth the*

*journey is just beginning. You have many more steps to take. Your life will influence the turning of history. I cannot tell you in what ways the future will unfold, but it is already written. Let this death only bring strength to your resolve, not weaken its foundation."*

And then, as if light itself was revealed, Lasiandra felt a surge throughout her being. She knew that the omnipotent spirit had entered her soul. And although the feeling lasted only a fraction of a second, her cells themselves were rejuvenated. The woman seemed to magically vanish, and Lasiandra found herself lying in a field that bordered the convent of the holy priestesses of the temple.

Three slaves had already died. Xerxes had been in a two day rage. He pounded the wall and broke furniture. Over the past 48 hours, the King of Kings had barely slept. Three times during that period he broke down sobbing like a child. One of the slaves died by trying to comfort the King as he sat in the royal garden with his hands on his head. The slave had come up behind the King and patted him on the back. Without notice, Xerxes swung around and grabbed the slave by the throat. His eyes were on fire as he lifted the slave off the ground by the neck. The slave gasped and began to struggle, but Xerxes was too powerful and blood started dripping from his neck where the King held him. The man tried to talk, but the King finally exerted his entire strength and an audible crack was heard as the man's neck was broken. Xerxes held the small man in the air for a few seconds then flung him across the area, where the dead slave landed in the flower garden, staining the white roses red. With no remorse, the King strode away leaving the dead slave lying in his own blood.

The reported loss of Hamas brought the young King of the vast Persian Empire to an emotional crisis. He relied on Hamas, he leaned on his experience. Losing him shook the King to his very core. He didn't previously realized how this loss would affect him. He never even considered that Hamas could be lost. He was invincible, and yet he is now gone. Where should he turn, who could he rely on?

The King retreated into a very dark emotional hole. He sank so low that he even considered ending his life. The pain of his loss was so great, crushing his very soul. This loss created the first emotional crisis for the young monarch. He needed help and he knew it. He needed to return to the caves; he needed his stepmother, Ho of Sebennytos.

Xerxes' stepmother, the Egyptian mystic that lived in a cave a few miles from the capital of Susa was one of the few people left for the Persian monarch, to confide in with implicitly trust. He felt a hole in his heart with the loss of Hamas. When the King entered the cave he was a different person than the last time he had visited. His stooped posture betrayed his emotional struggles. Although he walked, it almost appeared as though he crawled into the cave. Xerxes was a broken man. His legendary anger had transformed into a melancholy that was unmatched in his life. Inside his mind, Xerxes blamed himself for the death of his mentor, and it was a sin for which he could never forgive himself.

Ho of Sebennytos was a large woman. She was covered with many strange tattoos and her hair was shaved off the top of her head. But the King noticed nothing about his stepmother. He could only pay attention to his sorrow and grief. His mind was no longer open to the wonders of the world. He did not remember his trip to the cave. Tiamat, the internal monster, was slowly strangling the young monarch. The man who conquered the hungry lion, who faced every danger head on, unafraid of its outcome, was now a defeated soul, subjugated by an incident that happened over 1500 miles away. Ho stood and looked at the man sitting before her with his hands over his face weeping almost uncontrollably. If it wasn't for the facial recognition, she would not have known the man that whimpered before her was her stepson, Xerxes.

She approached him. The great King of Kings moved not an inch, did not acknowledge her presence, just continued to weep like an abandoned child. Ho gently placed her hand on the young King's head and slowly rubbed it in a circular fashion. Finally, after a brief period, Xerxes lifted his head to look at his stepmother. But as he did, and without warning, Ho lifted her right arm, slapping the King across his face. He fell from his stool onto the ground and, with a surprised and pleading expression, looked up at his stepmother. Ho said nothing but took a step toward the young King and kneeled in front of him.

*"There, now you feel real pain!"*

The King, still lying on the ground raised his hand to his reddened face, the stinging of the slap still radiating through his head.

*"Your tears will not return your friend!"*

*"But I killed him, mother, don't you understand?"*

*"Of course you didn't kill him. Circumstance did. From what I have heard, the King of Sparta slayed your friend."*

*"But I sent him, mother"*

*"My son, over the next few days I will teach you how to turn the pain around. You will learn to turn it, to direct it toward the real source of your sorrow. You will learn that the cure for your pain is revenge!"*

Now, kneeling on one knee, his face still wet from his tears, Xerxes responded to his mother.

*"Will the revenge take away the emptiness I feel in my chest?"*

*"No, my son, that is a sign of the love that you felt for Hamas"*

She now reached down and placed her hand under his chin, lifting it up slowly to stare into her blood red eyes.

*"You will learn, Xerxes, to turn sorrow into anger. You must allow the sorrow to ignite the rage that lies within you and direct it outward, not in toward yourself. It is the world that creates the sorrow, my son, and you must learn to direct your response to those responsible"*

Ho hesitated and then sat next to her son.

*"Xerxes, I remember a story you told me about Hamas and shooting the bow. Do you remember the lesson?"*

*"Yes mother."*

*"Tell it to me, Xerxes"*

*"I was shooting at a target and hitting the center with every shot. I was very proud of myself for the skill I had developed."*

*"Go on."*

*"Hamas stood and laughed at me. He said, "You show me no skill, my young soon-to- be-King."*

*"No skill, I protested, I hit the center with every shot."*

*"He laughed again and said, "Come with me."*

*"He took me to a small tree near where we were standing. He had me climb up on a small branch that almost gave way under my weight. I was very unsteady and the branch rocked under my feet"*

*"And then, what, Xerxes?"*

*"Hamas had moved the target, and standing on the branch he asked me to shoot an arrow into the target. I had trouble balancing, and when I shot I missed the target completely."*

Xerxes now gave a half smile and continued, *"Hamas laughed again at me. Then he said, "Anyone can hit a target on steady ground. The key to life is hitting the target when the ground moves under your feet."*

Now Ho smiled. She patted her son on the shoulder. *"Xerxes, the ground has moved under your feet. It is now time to learn how to hit the real target."*

The next few days were very difficult for the young King. He had to learn a new way of living. He had to vanquish his inner monster and learn to turn his pain around. But after the training from his stepmother, the King emerged from the cave a new man. He had learned the pain of loss and acquired the knowledge of how to allow it to fortify him, not deprive him of his strength. Pain had to be captured and reemerge into motivation and lust for revenge. He learned how to live and survive in an unsteady world. He shed some of the simplicities of his youth and faced the harshness of the realities.

Xerxes left the cave standing tall, solidly upright. His jaw was clenched and his eyes were refocused. Two days later Xerxes traveled almost three miles northeast of Susa to a temple that his father, Darius, had built in honor of the God Ahuramazda. There were three prayers that were essential to reach the God; Ahura Vairya, Ashem-vohu and Airyema-ishyo. Xerxes began with a personal prayer:

*"The Kingdom of Ahura brings all of life's deeds together. May the search for righteousness lead me to Ahuramazda. I proclaim you, Ahuramazda, to be the one God that rules all other fake deities. Please, God, send me what I desire. In your good kingdom we will partake in the glory of your strength."*

Xerxes began chanting silently. The song lasted exactly seven minutes, as he bent in prayer, rocking back and forth in a repetitious fashion. This hymn marked the beginning of the three day fast that involved bloodletting and self-flagellation.

Xerxes emerged from the fast reenergized. He had been mourning his teacher Hamas for the past number of days. As he beat his back, he castigated himself for sending Hamas to Delphi. And now he was gone, dead in a foreign province. He couldn't even recover the dead body. He barely had the volitional control to keep his anger in control. He had a blood vengeance vow against Athens to avenge his father, but now this feeling went beyond anger, it had reached fury. He just didn't want to kill the Greeks, he wanted to punish them. He wanted to taste their blood and burn their holy city of Athens to the ground. Xerxes looked to the heavens. More so, he was told that the Spartan King, Leonidas, had murdered Hamas. He was told that Hamas was surprised and ambushed by twenty-five Spartan soldiers. Hamas first tried to negotiate with the King and then bravely defended himself. The spy went on to say that the Spartan King removed the head of Hamas to return it to his city as a sign of his victory and superiority over the Spartan civilization. The spy who relayed this story to the Persian monarch died for its retelling. Xerxes had lost control during the details. He couldn't wash the image of his teacher's head sitting atop a pole outside of Sparta. He saw the blood dripping down the pole and the Spartan laughing and pointing to the dead body part.

*"I swear, my father. When I arrive at Athens, nothing will be left breathing, nothing. No animal, no bird, no bug, and no human. I will burn every plant and destroy every insect that roams the ground. I will drench the ground red, and shit on their bones. I swear it, my father! I swear it, my teacher!"*

He threw down the staff he was carrying and walked out of the temple. Tears were gone. There was nothing more to say now, only to do was left.

Eudox was not happy. It was now apparent that there was no way to stop the Persian invasion. Although he would never give voice to it, he didn't believe that the shaky Greek alliance could withstand the onslaught. He was not confident in Themistocles' idea that they should empty Athens of the populace, dividing the women and children between the city of Troezen and the island of Salamis. A preposterous notion in Eudox' mind. He just couldn't imagine the enormity of the task. And the entire male population would man the boats. Farmers, berry pickers, potters, artists, all manning the boats? It was ridiculous. Maybe the army, or the hoplites, or the cavalry could learn the skill. After all, they were all in good physical condition. But the sheep herders, the wine merchants, the tailors, how could they compete against a well-trained Persian navy?

But, Eudox reasoned to himself, even if this rag-tag conglomeration of men could learn to coordinate their movements, even if they could magically develop the physical prowess to unendingly row for hours at a time, even if the Greek admirals out think their Persian counterparts, they would still be outnumbered between four and eight to one. Unimaginable odds. Not only could they not defend against such numbers, how could they defeat them?

Eudox had a headache that pounded over the entirety of his skull. He was ashamed of his thoughts. Fleetingly he planned how to escape the Persian horde if they overran the Greek cities. Could he escape by land or by sea? Should he secure some escape route when he returned to Athens? A chill ran down his back as he contemplated the possibilities. He saw the strength of his close confident, Themistocles. He was self-assured in his decisions, and Eudox believed that the father of the Demos wholeheartedly believed that the Greek alliance would succeed. Many nights Eudox felt a coward.

As he rode in the cart on the return trip to Athens, Eudox was dizzy with fear and consternation. Then he realized that Themistocles' defense guaranteed the destruction of Athens. Abandoning the city to the King of Kings meant everything burning to the ground. He envisioned it. He could see in his mind's eye the temples in ashes, the beautiful causeways chopped into rubble, the end of everything that he knew and loved. Of course, he couldn't disagree with Themistocles. He trusted him more than any person he ever knew. But this, this strategy was recklessness and bordered on rashness. The Greek hoplites defeated the Persian at Marathon and they were outnumbered there. And now Themistocles abandons the hoplites, turns them into sailors. He is abandoning our proven strength in favor of what? A feeling, a hope, what? This is craziness. In many ways, Eudox the man dedicated to Themistocles, believed in the strategy of his political rival, Aristides. The man that Eudox trusted with his life, all of a sudden seemed to lose his senses. What should he do? His world had been shaken. All of sudden, what he thought was true and dependable did not appear such. Everything was becoming real very quickly. The ground that he depended on to be steady and flat, was suddenly slippery and foggy. He could no longer see the future. What he saw was all bad. He could not even imagine a positive outcome.

Eudox' shame was palpable. After all the challenges that he had tackled over the years, after all the hurdles that stood in his way and were overcome. What he had feared since the beginning had become true. He had lost his faith.

Sakarbaal  sat on the dock and watched the beautiful new triremes. He had come to love the city of Athens, the new harbor complex at Piraeus, and for that matter, Themistocles himself. When he first agreed to this arrangement he didn't consider himself to be a political person. He thought he could take a blind eye and not care about the job he was asked to do. He knew in his heart he was Phoenician and would always be such. He knew from the beginning there was a hidden agenda. But over the past few months he began to realize that he was infatuated by this place.

Sakarbaal had never really had much responsibility in his life. He was always a superior sailor and he considered himself an adequate strategist. But here he had supervised the most expansive building operation that he could imagine. He also trained sailors and captains and taught an aggressive attack and defense strategy. Sakarbaal was honestly proud of his accomplishments.

As he sat assessing his situation, his thoughts returned to the first time he met Themistocles. He thought to himself, *"A deceitful and cunning man. There was no clarity in the man. Everything was hidden, covered in shadows. It was like trying to see someone through a dense, morning fog. I must be careful, more than I ever was."*

Sakarbaal had come to Greece on a trading mission with Yutpan, and Baido the negotiator. Their goal was to secure a trading relationship with Athens, or so he forced himself to believe. Sakarbaal remembered when he was questioned by Themistocles before he was dealt to the Greek for the promise of trade. He had developed a close relationship with this man, and now he wondered if he lied to him from the beginning. When Themistocles asked about The Warrior Queen, Sakarbaal didn't lie, but he also didn't tell the entire truth. He said he knew the Queen and knew of her superlative reputation. What he didn't say was that he considered her undefeatable. He had known the Warrior Queen since his early adulthood. She could defeat any two men. He had seen her, without remorse, butcher many enemies. She was quick tempered, but her emotions didn't seem to interfere or affect her decision making. But now that he thought about this, he felt that it was it was Themistocles who lied. He had made an oft comment that he was afraid of the ocean. Sakarbaal never forgot that comment. He soon found out what an untruth it was. Themistocles was not only comfortable in the water, but he would lead the Athenian and Greek navy against the Persian. Over the course of his stay here in Athens, he silently caught Themistocles in many more lies.

Sakarbaal stared out into the Aegean as his mind drifted to many subjects. He knew that with all the deception that Themistocles put forward, it was nothing in comparison to his own. He recalled the meeting with King Matten, the Phoenician monarch, when this venture was being planned. He walked into the holy temple where the King sat and was anxious with anticipation. It was a great honor to be called before Matten. He had met the King only a few times and he was about to find out how much the King actually knew about him. He remembered bowing with one knee touching the ground.

*"Sakarbaal, I am glad you chose to answer my call."*

Matten rose as he spoke.

*"My lord, you have only to ask and my devotion will lead me to complete whatever task you lay out for me. It is my destiny to serve you."*

*"Excellent,"* Matten said.

*"Sakarbaal, I understand that you speak fluent Greek."*

*"Yes, lord. I learned it as a child when I worked for a Corinthian trader."*

*"I have also heard of your stellar reputation as a man of strength. In your many adventures you have proven your heroic nature."*

*"Thank you, lord."*

Sakarbaal bowed his head once more. He flushed with pride that the King held him in such high esteem.

*"Sakarbaal, I have a task for you, a very dangerous task,"* Matten said, immediately becoming more serious.

*"I obey your words, my King,"* Sakarbaal replied in genuine reverence.

*"This task will take every portion of your skill. You will need to act a part and betray new found friends. You will need to make believe that you are someone you are not, and if found out, you will lose your life."*

*"A life lost in service of my King and my people is a courageous death. I seek such an end,"* Sakarbaal spoke.

Matten responded, *"Good, Sakarbaal, good. Your people will owe you a great debt, and your family will be honored for generations."*

The King became pensive. Again he turned to his loyal subject. He stared for a moment at the sailor, as if trying to determine how much he should actually reveal. Finally, his facial expression changed and he said, *"Sakarbaal, I must tell you the truth. Our spies have told us that the head of the Greek Demos is looking to build a functional navy. They hope to build new ships and create a navy to fight the Persians. They cannot do it alone, they will need help."*

The sailor continued to stare at his King. He couldn't really believe what he was hearing. The King continued, *"They will need help, Sakarbaal... you will be that help."*

Sakarbaal's task was straightforwardly outlined to him by the King. He was to swear allegiance to Athens and help their leader, Themistocles, to build and train a navy. It was an ironic twist of fate that Themistocles actually asked for his services in return for the trade agreement.

*"The sheep opened the door for the fox to enter,"*

Sakarbaal quietly laughed to himself. This Themistocles was reputed to be such a shrewd man, and yet he sealed his own fate, asking for the spy to be let into his inner circle.

*"Remarkable,"* Sakarbaal thought.

And the Phoenician sailor had done what he promised. He built the Athenian navy. He trained this navy and set up a communication system for them to use during war. As he did this, he snuck out in the middle of many nights to convey the information he was compiling about this new navy to Phoenician spies. But now came the hardest task given to Sakarbaal. During his last meeting with his Phoenician contact he was told that he had to devise a way to sabotage the navy he had supervised building. Matten wanted the Persian King to have another advantage in his attack of Athens. Such a help would cement the King of King's indebtedness to the Phoenician state. But more than that, Matten wanted Sakarbaal to kill Themistocles.

The old priest was now so ancient he could hardly move on his own. Even though he was still a man of consequence, he now needed help to accomplish many of the simplest feats of life. He stood with help and walked only with support. Sometimes when he moved he would lose his balance and would teeter on falling. Ningizzida had six personal acolytes. All these young men were devoted heart and soul to the old man. None of them questioned his decisions. His reputation and the stories about his 'miracles' were so well known that there were some sects that worshiped him directly as God's messenger on earth. It was rumored that he could heal those afflicted and curse those whom strayed from the course of the truth.

It had been told that the priest visited people in their dreams. It was said that non-believers and people who had strayed from the spoken word were at risk for nightly visits from the ethereal priest. Many people suffering from sickness also reported dream visits from Ningizzida. Such reports spread fear throughout communities. It was such rumors, and the fear of godly retribution, that kept many of the flock in line.

But with all his devotions and piety, Ningizzida was obsessed. One nagging desire controlled his thoughts. Every day he taught the religious dogmas and the secrets of the old ways. After all, he was the Sheshgallu, the guardian of the holy rituals and prayers. Many times during his preaching Ningizzida would fall into old languages to present his revelations. His acolytes would beg the priest to speak in ways they could understand. Ningizzida would seem lost for a moment then return to speaking Babylonian.

Ningizzida understood the pure Apsu- that sacred space that connected the God, Marduk, with all organisms. Furthermore, he was learned in the Enuma Elish. These seven tablets of creation held many of the secrets of immortality. For many hours Ningizzida would teach his students how to read the holy smoke and interpret what Marduk wanted of his people.

Most men were controlled by their inner monster, Tiamat. Tiamat was that energy that flowed through all people and continually tried to overcome and control the person. Many times during one's lifetime, the monster attempted to engulf the soul. Few of us have the strength to defeat the monster or keep it at bay. He haunts the night and plays on our weaknesses and fears. In our hours of psychic frailty, the monster gains his strength. Only very few are strong enough to endure the continual attack from Tiamat.

THE DELPHIC ORACLE · 227

The priest not only endured, but he defeated the inner chaos, or so he thought.

However out of all his accomplishments, he could not rid himself of the desire for revenge on Xerxes. Tiamat was sneaky. For Ningizzida, the path to control of his mind rested in anger. The more hatred, the less control he had. He lived in his desire for revenge. It was the way the monster, Tiamat, haunted him. More times than he could imagine he tried to rid himself of the desire for retaliation. But his mind was stuck in a never ending spiritual darkening. The more he tried, the stronger the desire became and the more it embraced him. This desire was like quicksand. The more he struggled, the deeper he sank. What was more was that the old priest knew that many times he had the young within his grasp, but every time he made the decision to allow him escape. It reached the point where the anger at himself rivaled that against his adversary.

But Ningizzida fought death. Many times in his life he reached the footsteps of the dark temple. He couldn't allow his demise until he had had his retribution. This desire was the food that kept him moving. It provided enough emotional nourishment to starve death itself.

Artemisia and her entourage of Phoenician guards rode hard for two days. Their goal was to reach one of the northern Greek cities that had already given the King of Kings the water and dirt. The acceptance of water and dirt was the traditional Persian expression of submission to the will of the King. When the Persian diplomat arrived in Sparta demanding the water and dirt, he was unceremoniously thrown in a pit and stoned to death. The Athenians were somewhat more civilized, rejecting the overture but allowing the diplomat to retain his life. In both instances, the

King of Kings fell into a rage of unknown proportions. He had made the offer to Athens in spite of the animosity he had for Marathon. To be rejected outright by these upstart Greeks was an insult he could not swallow. He could feel the bile burning in his throat. And whenever it seemed to settle, the slave reminded him to, 'Remember Marathon.'

Artemisia and the Phoenicians were headed to the northern part of Attica. They were headed to Macedonia which had already Medonized. The Macedonian King had become a staunch ally of Xerxes. The Warrior Queen had reasoned that she and the Phoenicians would stay with their allied King until Xerxes arrived with the invasion force.

The Warrior Queen was proud of her stay at Delphi. She stood up to the Greek God and slew his messenger. There was no consequence; she was not struck down by Apollo. Even the Gods were afraid of the Warrior Queen, she concluded. As she knew all along, the Greek Gods were an illusion, something made up by man to delude him into mistaken belief. Further, these Greeks were such a stupid people, believing in this strange Demos over the Persian order. How could they believe that the Persian King would not rule the world? How could they believe that the masses could rule a country? What kind of concept was letting the lower classes decide on the fate of the city or the Empire? This fatal flaw would eventually destroy the Athenian state and their fledgling Demos. Once the Persian invasion occurred, and when the people saw the strength of the Persian might, Artemisia believed they would voluntarily abandon these ludicrous concepts in favor of the accepted, traditional order. With an enlightened monarch like Xerxes guiding the destiny of the superior race, the end result of this conflict was pre-determined, and for that matter preferred.

Artemisia was excited with anticipation. The invasion was now a forgone conclusion. She could wait in Macedonia and the army would come to her. She would take control of the Persian navy and sail south to destroy the Greeks. It had been a long time since Artemisia had been in a conflict of any magnitude. But this, this would be a glorious encounter. The urge and the longing that the Warrior Queen felt was greater than any physical need could be. She was transfixed into a semiconscious state as she reveled in the possibilities of the future. As she rode her mind was filled with the expectation of strategy, of attack, of the men screaming and falling overboard. Drowning, gasping for air, she could see their pleading eyes, desperate to hold onto life, yet with no hope of rescue. Artemisia felt goose bumps and warmth in her body as she envisioned the carnage. As she rode she rubbed her thighs against the horse until enormous pleasure rose and exploded in orgasm. The two feelings, that of death and sexual satisfaction, had merged into one concept. The Queen screamed with delight as her legs weakened and her body spasmed. Her screams were drowned out by the sound of the horses beating their trail over the hardened ground. Others looked at her in surprise when she yelled to the clouds. They thought she was just lost in her own revelry.

Both Gods were forlorn. It had never happened before in recorded history. A mortal had brutally murdered the Pythia. Apollo had never considered such a possibility. With all his infinite wisdom and his ability to peer into the future, he had not foreseen this tragedy. It was a sign. He realized that his skills and insights were diminishing. After many millenniums, the God was losing his omnipotence. It was dissolving before his eyes. Gods were not usually surprised. They knew the future before it was a thought in man's mind. His head bowed, he looked at Athena.

*"What is happening to us?"* Apollo asked in a sheepish fashion.

*"Faith has been lost!"* Athena said, as she looked down through the clouds.

*"We have no power without belief. We are infused with supremacy. Every temple, every prayer, every sacrifice, leads to our command. Without the love and devotion of people, our essences evaporate."*

Apollo raised his head.

*Why has this happened?"*

Athena looked at him with a smile

*"Our children have grown. They have decided that their belief in themselves is more important than their belief in us. They no longer believe in their parental Gods."*

A tear emerged from Apollo's eyes. Athena commented, *"A tear my brother, I have never seen you cry."*

Apollo looked up at Athena. He turned his head as he looked around.

*Where is Bubo?"*

*"He's already gone, Apollo. He has joined the immortality of energy. I will miss him."*

The building was old and the walls were cracked. When it rained the ceiling leaked with the water mixing with the sludge and rocks of the floor. There was mud on the floor and the patrons were mostly poor men who vomited and urinated on the ground as their intoxication increased. The smell in the room was that of putrid human excrement. Most of the patrons had no teeth and their clothes smelled almost as badly as the men themselves. Many would sleep the night in this place in their own vomit and urine. Cats and mice ignoring each other roamed freely across the floor.

This was the eighth place that the captain had visited. It was by far the most disgusting. He almost passed it by because of the reputation and the obvious stench that this establishment held. Thantos could not believe that his patron could have ended up in such a place. The building was in the poorest section of Athens, and, after dark, was generally avoided by most of the population. As the captain entered the room he held his nose and gingerly stepped across the room. Thoroughly disgusted, Thantos almost turned and left. But he decided that this would be his last visit to an inn this night, so a few more seconds of search was called for. As he entered the center of the establishment his eyes drifted to a corner on his left. The man lying on the floor with his arm resting of the back wall, and his robe pulled up around his waist revealing his mud and excrement stained ass and legs looked vaguely familiar. Thantos walked over two others lying still in the center of the room. He leaned over the man and smiled as he identified Themistocles snoring in the corner.

As Thantos walked to his friend, he stood over him and smiled to himself. His thoughts were mixed with tragedy and irony.

*"We are facing the largest and most sophisticated army ever assembled. Our enemies number closer to the hundred thousand and our own support is puny in comparison. The Athenian navy is infantile, and the Persian outnumbered us almost ten to one. There are enemies and spies in every ally and street of the city. The great Oracle at Delphi predicted destruction for our beloved city and for our culture as well. What was the strategy that Themistocles reasoned in* response *to this invasion? It was to abandon the city of all the woman and children, and take all the farmers and tradesmen to man the ships. And the leader of this great navy who would repel the Persians from Attica, lay on the floor in his own vomit in the most disgusting building of the entire city."*

As he stared at the leader of the Demos, Thantos silently reminisced about the different experiences that he had in service of Athens and the great Greek strategist, Themistocles. He remembered the kidnapping of the young girl by his pirate compatriot, Ptea. He had manipulated the Corinthian ship builder, Cratinus, by kidnapping his daughter. Thantos managed to secure the triremes from Cratinus by 'saving' his daughter from the bloodthirsty pirates. He smiled to himself remembering the rouse. Thantos looked again at the man lying in front of him. This is the man who possessed the metis. The metis, the visionary gift that the Goddess Athena gave to certain mortals. Odysseus possessed the ability. The metis was the God-given ability to lead others by charisma. One who possessed this mysterious ability could anticipate trouble and decisions would be guided by divine intervention. And here he lay. The man who supposedly possessed the metis. He lay naked with his ass covered in mud and urine.

A cloud seemed to cover Thantos' soul as he remembered Phecontalis. Phecontalis was his loyal lieutenant who was murdered by the Persians as he waited to return Thantos to Attica. Thantos had accompanied three Greek spies to scout the Persian military strength. The three men sent to investigate the Persians did not survive the journey. Thantos was the only survivor of the adventure. Phecontalis was probably the only man that Thantos loved. He swore that he would live long enough to avenge his friend. He knew that in the upcoming war, many battles would be played out on the sea, and he swore he would be there to aide in the cause and punish the Persian. He hoped beyond hope that he would meet the Persian general in combats, the man who had brutally murdered Phecontalis.

Thantos knew that the odds were that neither he, nor Themistocles, would survive this upcoming war. This was not like the conflict with Aegina. That was a conflict of attrition that had lasted almost a decade. This new war would be fast and decisive. If the Athenians lost, it meant genocide. But at this time, Thantos didn't really care. He had joined the cause for the adventure and the monetary gain. He would stay involved to bloody the nose of an enemy and revenge his friend. Even if the enemy eventually took his life, he would die happily knowing that his sword was buried in the heart of his enemy. He would fight for revenge.

Thantos bent down and started to lift his drunken friend. It was not an easy task, as Themistocles vomited on his shirt during the process. Thantos took out a number of rags that he carried for this exact purpose. But the sailor did not wipe the vomit from his body. He began wiping the dirt and urine from his friend's face and shoulders. He put Themistocles' arm around his shoulder and

234 · JEFFREY DONNER

slowly began to walk to the door. His friend reeked of feces and other smells he could not identify. But it mattered not to the sailor.

The two men staggered to the door. The drunken politician and the tired and worn out sailor made a strange sight. One man had spent his life smuggling wine and other delicacies throughout the Greek world, and the other, an impulsive, gambling usurer, who had risen to the head of the city, was the champion of an audacious and unlikely political experiment called a Demos. Such an approach had never been tried or proposed before. Solon, Themistocles' hero, had freed the poor from their economic slavery. And now Themistocles aimed to set the course of government away from tyranny to participatory democracy. The dye had been cast; the Persians were already on the march, and this experimental democracy would most likely die in infancy.

As the two men reached the door the sun was already rising in the east. The light blinded Thantos. He squinted and looked to the horizon. He turned to Themistocles who was trying to open his eyes. The politician moved his free hand to his head, suggesting the pain that throbbed though his temples. Thantos patted him on his back and said, *"You have had your play, my friend. The Persians are coming to visit and I don't think they will be very polite."*

Themistocles blew gas and almost fell on his face. Thantos laughed again as he repositioned the politician on his shoulder.

*"We will need more than a big smell from your ass to survive my friend."*

The men took a few more steps. Again Thantos looked at his friend.

*"No more drink, my friend. It is time to save Athens. It is time to save our people. It is time to save the Demos."*

As the two men walked away from the saloon, the sound of thunder rang through the sky. A storm was appearing on the horizon.

Thantos looked at the horizon and thought, *"The sun is coming up, but is it rising on the Persian Empire or the fledgling Demos? "*

His shoulders began to ache, as the weight of his friend began pressing on his bones. Many things had changed in his life over the past number of months. He almost couldn't believe that the drunk that he carried was the man who held the lives of so many in his hand. Could he ever understand Themistocles? Probably not, he concluded. Compared to the Greek politician, Thantos' life was simple, direct. The old sailor looked out over the docks. The rising sun shone on the waves as he slowly walked out of the bar with his friend on his shoulder. Thantos stopped and put his friend down on a small bench. He continued to walk toward the water line and ended up staring out over the Aegean. The world was changing. He looked around, back at his friend and knew in his heart that soon nothing he knew would be recognizable. He tried to imprint images on his mind. Thantos recalled the Persian army and navy that he witnessed. Tears came to his eyes as the realization of the devastation and carnage loomed over the horizon. The Persians would burn this city to the ground. His friend, and probably he, himself, would both be dead within the year. And no matter how clever or lucky, the future was foretold by the Oracle. Black blood. Thantos swallowed hard. He looked at his friend snoring next to him and silently promised that he would not run. Armageddon was coming, but he would not run.

# End of Book III of the Great Persian Saga

The Great Persian Saga continues
in the last book of the series …

BOOK IV: THE GREAT PERSIAN SAGA

# PRAY TO THE WIND

## ARMAGEDDON

A NOVEL BY

## DR. JEFFREY DONNER

PRAY TO THE WIND

www.ingramcontent.com/pod-product-compliance
Lightning Source LLC
Chambersburg PA
CBHW060019100426
42740CB00010B/1527